STRIKE PREVENTION AND CONTROL HANDBOOK

Robert W. Mulcahy
and Marion C. Smith

of

Mulcahy & Wherry, S.C.
815 East Mason Street
Milwaukee, Wisconsin
53202-4080
414-278-7110

Executive Enterprises Publications Co., Inc.
New York

This publication is designed to provide accurate and authorative information regarding its subject matter. It is sold with the understanding that the publisher is not engaged in rendering legal, accounting or other professional service. If legal advice or other expert assistance is required, the services of a competent professional person should be sought. --From a Declaration of Principles jointly adopted by a Committee of the American Bar Association and a Committee of Publishers.

Be advised the authors could not address the legal aspects associated with specific state laws and statutes within the confines of this book. Accordingly, the authors do not assume any legal responsibility for state law which may contravene any legal analysis contained herein.

ISBN 0-88057-065-2
Library of Congress Catalog Card No. 83-82094

ABOUT THE AUTHORS

<u>Robert W. Mulcahy</u> is a graduate of Marquette University, College of Business Administration and a graduate of Marquette University Law School. He previously served as a trial attorney for the National Labor Relations Board. Mr. Mulcahy retains membership in the American, Wisconsin, and Milwaukee Bar Associations. He is also a Director of the Labor Law Section of the State Bar of Wisconsin. He is the co-author of an article in the <u>Labor Law Journal</u> entitled, "Trends in Hospital Labor Relations." Mr. Mulcahy also co-authored a related article entitled "Strikes: Strategy and Tactics for Managers" as published in the <u>Employee Relations Law Journal</u>. Mr. Mulcahy is a partner in the firm and specializes exclusively in labor relations at the firm of Mulcahy & Wherry, S.C., Milwaukee, Wisconsin.

<u>Marion Cartwright Smith</u> is a Phi Beta Kappa graduate of Marquette University and serves as Director of the Research Center at the law firm of Mulcahy & Wherry, S.C. She specializes in private and public sector labor relations. Marion Smith is a member of the Industrial Relations Research Association, and TEMPO (Business & Professional Womens Organization). Marion Smith serves on the Heritage Bank Financial Council and the Advisory Committee to Public Expenditure Committee of Wisconsin. She was a contributing author to <u>Municipal Labor Relations in Wisconsin</u> and co-author of the articles, "Last Best Offer, How to Win and Lose," as well as "Problems and Solutions Resulting from Inability to Pay in the Public Sector."

<u>Mulcahy & Wherry, S.C.</u> provides legal services to a variety of management clients throughout the State of Wisconsin and the nation from offices located in Eau Claire, Green Bay, Madison, Milwaukee, Oshkosh and Wausau. Mulcahy & Wherry, S.C. represents private sector employers, counties, municipalities and schools, thereby offering its clients services that encompass virtually all aspects of labor/ management relations. A special thanks and appropriate recognition is given to Michael L. Roshar and Peter N. Hoeft of our office who were extensively involved with this project.

Table of Contents

FOREWARD

The threat of a strike is a union's most powerful weapon against an employer. A successful strike can cripple an employer from both an economic and public relations standpoint. Location, size, conditions of work, increased pay and benefits - none of these factors offer a guarantee against a strike action.

However, management is not helpless when confronted with a work stoppage. The employer can effectively defuse the impact of a strike by careful and thorough planning. This book is written to aid managers in devising a successful strike prevention and control plan to counter the threat and initiation of a strike.

Once the employee organization initiates a work stoppage it is much too late to begin planning. By that time, the union will have brought in professionals to coordinate the strike. State and national employee organizations provide both financial help for striking employees and experts in bargaining, strike organization and public relations. A management strike team that has not planned far in advance will not be able to combat these forces. The time to start preparing is now.

The authors bring to this work the background of substantial experience and expertise in labor relations. Each
author has been extensively involved in collective bargaining negotiations and the preparation of strike plans. This
book serves as a practical reference guide for action in
successfully preventing and controlling a strike.

Lewis Abrams
Publisher
Executive Enterprises
    Publications Co., Inc.

STRIKE PREVENTION
AND CONTROL
HANDBOOK

I. INTRODUCTION

The threat of a strike often presents management with
greater problems than the problems posed by the strike
itself. Because of management's uncertainty as to how to
legally and effectively cope with a strike and it's potential impact, the threat of a strike is the most powerful
weapon in the union's arsenal. This book is intended to
apprise management of the need to make strike preparations
and the specific factors and concerns that should be
addressed in developing and coordinating a strike plan.[1]

Once the strike hits, it can be too late to effectively
cope because the battle lines for the conflict have already
been drawn. Management should take prompt and decisive
action before the strike to effectively deal with its
impact. Immediate tasks must be undertaken to minimize the
effect of the walkout and to support company morale.

---

[1] Please note that all references to "men" or related
pronouns such as "his" or "he" are used solely for literary
purposes and are meant in their generic sense to include
all humankind.

Indecision, confusion, and hesitancy, which frequently
result from the failure to plan in advance, could fore-
shadow ultimate capitulation to labor's demands. The
material in this book should help management formulate a
plan that will insure a successful resolution of the
strike. Since the strike is economic warfare, management
must develop a strategy to understand and counter the union
tactics.

II. SETTING THE SCENE FOR THE STRIKE

A. What Causes Strikes?

On the surface, there are several major reasons why a
union calls a strike. These reasons include wage and benefit disputes, union recognition and security, job security
and/or work rule disputes, disputes over relocation of work
or subcontracting, as well as self-help strikes over alleged
grievances. However, there are more subtle reasons why a
strike eventually does or does not come to fruition. One
factor involves the influence of the employer's behavior on
the union's propensity to take strike action. Other
factors may include anti-union conduct by a company, the
quality of a management decision, the methods used to

explain decisions, the employer's misjudgment of the political environment within a bargaining unit or the bargaining process itself.

These factors combined with the forces operative within the union may contribute greatly to the atmosphere within which a strike is possible, if not inevitable. The influence of the union's internal politics on the strike vote may be difficult for all but the most intuitive observer to predict. The inability of the union leadership to control or influence its membership as well as competition among union leaders may contribute greatly to the probability of a strike. These situations are difficult for an employer to effectively influence, much less control. A combination of many of these factors often weighs heavily when decisions to call a strike are made by union memberships.

Appendix A provides a breakdown of work stoppages in 1983 by region, union affiliation and industry. As the economy turns upward, strikes are once again a frequent occurrence. Unions are fighting back from a serious recession. Union membership and dues fell off considerably. Union staff cuts curbed union organizing and strike activity. The unions have been forced to concede takebacks in the course of concession bargaining. The unions have waited their turn and they are poised for action. There have been significant strikes in a wide variety of industries from coast to coast.

B. Background Information and Definitions.

A strike is quite simply a cessation of work by employees in an effort to obtain or maintain favorable terms of employment. A strike does not necessarily terminate the employer-employee relationship. The courts have held that employees have a vested property interest in the right to strike and that this right is protected by the Fourteenth Amendment and may not be denied without due process of law. The law does not, however, treat all strikes the same way. The initial and most important determination an employer must make is the proper classification of the strike. Management can then recognize and formulate various strategies to legally and practically deal with the strike, determine whether to seek the intervention of the National Labor Relations Board (NLRB) and assess the employer's potential exposure. While there are several types of strikes distinguishable on the factors that motivate them, strikes may be generally classified as "protected" or "non-protected." Non-protected strikes, in turn, may be prohibited (illegal) or non-prohibited (merely unprotected). Unprotected strikes may be prohibited actions either because their substantive purpose is not lawful or because the means used by the strikers are illegal.

The rights of employees to engage in protected strike activities is protected by statute and by case law. Section 7 of the National Labor Relations Act (hereinafter NLRA) guarantees employees the right "to engage in other concerted activities for the purpose of collective bargaining or other mutual aid or protection."[2/] This provision protects the right to strike so long as it is within the statutory protection. Two forms of strikes are permissible as protected under the NLRA: economic strikes and unfair labor practice (ULP) strikes.

[2/] SEC. 7. Employees shall have the right to self-organization, to form, join, or assist labor organizations, to bargain collectively through representatives of their own choosing, and to engage in other concerted activities for the purpose of collective bargaining or other mutual aid or protection, and shall also have the right to refrain from any or all of such activities except to the extent that such right may be affected by an agreement requiring membership in a labor organization as a condition of employment as authorized in section 8(a)(3). (See Appendix B for the full text of the NLRA.)

The most important reason for distinguishing between the different types of strikes is that the determination of the strike's legality will also determine the job rights of the strikers. Strikers engaged in protected activity may not be discharged but they may be replaced during the strike. Usually, unprotected strikers may be discharged and need not be rehired after the strike. Not all unprotected strikers, however, are necessarily illegal strikers. Defining the type of strike can be a very complex area of the Federal law.

1.   Economic Strikes.

An economic strike is an action taken as a pressure tactic to secure more advantageous wages, benefits or working conditions. Case law has defined the economic strike in the negative as "a lawful or protected strike not caused by an unfair labor practice." An economic strike is a protected strike under Section 7 of the NLRA. Employees who participate in an economic strike do not lose their employee status. An employer may not discharge economic strikers simply because they have participated in an economic strike.

On the other hand, an employer is free to operate his business during an economic strike. In order to maintain his operations, an employer may hire temporary or permanent replacements. It is not an unfair labor practice to refuse to discharge persons hired to replace economic strikers. An employer, however, must reinstate economic strikers, or place them on a preferential rehire list, if they make an unconditional offer to return to work. This means that returning strikers, or the union on their behalf, must make an "unconditional offer" to return to work in order to ensure the strikers' continued employee status. The mere termination of the strike is not a guarantee of continued employment for these workers. An employer has a legal duty to immediately reinstate employees who offer to return if their positions are still open. If no position is available the economic striker is placed on a preferential rehire list.

2. Unfair Labor Practice Strikes.

An unfair labor practice strike is a strike which is precipitated by proven unfair labor practices, even if the unfair labor practices were only a contributing factor to the strike. Examples are strikes protesting an employer's refusal to bargain in good faith or his discriminatory discharge of an employee. Mere allegations (charges) of unfair labor practices do not, however, form a basis for finding the existence of an unfair labor practice strike. The law clearly provides that there must be proof of a causal relationship between the violation of the NLRA and the strike.

Management must exercise the greatest caution in handling unfair labor practice strikes. Few strikes actually are found to be unfair labor practice strikes by the NLRB. When an unfair labor practice strike is found, however, the Board will become involved and the liability can be substantial. Unfair labor practice strikers are entitled to immediate reinstatement (i.e., within five days of their unconditional offer to return to work). There is no recourse to a preferential rehire list for these strikers. If necessary, an employer must replace employees who were hired to take the positions of the strikers in order to reinstate the returning people. These strikers are afforded the greatest protection under the NLRA.

3. <u>Unprotected Strikes.</u>

Any strike action taken by employees that does not conform to the provisions of NLRA Section 7 is not protected
by law. A common example of an unprotected strike is a
"wildcat" strike. A "wildcat" strike is an effort by a
group of employees to interfere with the duly authorized
collective bargaining agent's representation of the
employees. The strike is unprotected only when the
group's actions contravene the union's objectives. Since
the "wildcat" strike occurs during the term of the
contract, these strikers normally forfeit any protection
under the NLRA. "Wildcat" strikers may be terminated or
permanently replaced by an employer. Similarly, participation in a sit-down strike is clearly activity not
protected by the NLRA. So too, repeated refusals by
employees to perform <u>mandatory</u> overtime are normally unprotected as such activity constitutes a recurring or intermittent strike.

4. <u>Recognitional Strikes.</u>

A union may violate Section 8(b)(7) of the NLRA
(Appendix B) when that union pickets or threatens to picket

an employer. This picketing can be for the purpose of obtaining recognition as the bargaining representative of the company's employees or for the purpose of organizing those employees. This kind of picketing is prohibited if another union has been lawfully recognized by the picketed employer and no question of representation can be raised. This form of picketing is also outlawed if a valid election has been conducted within the preceding twelve months among the employees thought to be represented by the picketing union. If neither of the above conditions prevail, Section 8(b)(7)(C) permits such recognitional or organizational picketing for a reasonable period not to exceed 30 days without the filing of a representation petition. Once a petition has been filed, recognitional picketing can continue until a valid election has been held. It should be noted that this picketing is not legal merely because recognition is only one of the objects of the picketing. For example, picketing for recognition of a group of employees is not legal merely because it is also for informational purposes or has as its object protection of area working conditions.

5. Secondary Boycotts.

Section 8(b)(4)(B) of the National Labor Relations Act (NLRA) makes it an unfair labor practice for a union or its agent to engage in secondary boycotts. Secondary boycotts are perhaps most easily explained through the following example:

> A union has a dispute with Company A (primary employer). As an action in this dispute with Company A, the union forces or threatens Company B (supplier of Company A) to cease business with Company A. Company A is the primary employer and the union is free to strike Company A. Company B is the neutral or secondary employer. The union MAY NOT legally picket at Company B.

The union's goal in instituting a secondary boycott is to pressure and influence a secondary company to hurt the primary company with whom the union has the dispute. If allowed, a secondary boycott can be one of the most power-ful weapons in a union's arsenal. The primary/secondary distinction presupposes the existence of a neutral employer. The policy behind the law is to protect this innocent third party from concerted union activity over a dispute in which he is not involved. Secondary activity is normally illegal, therefore, unless the union is able to establish that the secondary company, which is the focus of this union pressure, is an "ally" of the primary company (i.e. not a neutral party to the dispute). The "ally doctrine" is rooted in the realization that in some cases one company constitutes an integral part of the operation of another company against whom a union has struck. The relationship between the two companies may result in an "alliance" under the law. The law has recognized two types of allied employers: 1) those who perform "farmed out" or subcontracted work which would have been performed by the primary employer but for the strike, and 2) those who share common ownership or management with the primary employer. The employer in the first category is said to be performing "struck work."

There are also several "alter ego" questions involved in the application of the ally doctrine. Under the "alter ego" doctrine, an employer who shares common ownership or management will be "placed in the shoes" of the primary employer. Accordingly, the union may boycott the secondary employer as an "alter ego" of the primary employer. Cases have been decided based on the determination of whether or not the same corporation has a plant in another state operating under a different name and management, whether a pre-existing agreement existed for the performance of struck work, whether the transferred work is the same type of work that was performed by the second plant before the strike, and whether the work transferred to the other plant is the same amount of work transferred before the strike or there has been an increase in the amount of work. Another element to be considered is whether the customer or the struck employer devised the system to farm out the "struck work." The specifics of these concerns need to be addressed before any of these options are implemented by the primary employer. Instead of minimizing the effects of the strike an employer may, by farming out work, actually increase the scope of the labor dispute. If the union can follow the struck work, the employer may be magnifying its own problems and those of fellow employers in the same industry.

6. Struck Work.

If a struck employer transfers bargaining unit work out which had not previously been subcontracted to another employer, such workload shall generally be catagorized as "struck work." In other words, struck work is work which a struck employer would ordinarily perform, but is unable or unwilling to perform because of a labor dispute. The legal consequence of such action is that the union may picket the employer to whom the work is contracted out. Over the years a body of case law has developed which indicates that the employer to whom work was farmed out, regardless of whether he is unionized or non-unionized, will be considered an "ally" of the struck employer. The legal consequences of this activity are that the union will be free to picket, with impunity, the employer who is performing the struck work without fear that such picketing violates the secondary boycott provisions of the NLRA. It has been held that any employer whose employees are performing work which would normally have been performed by the striking employees is an "ally" of the struck employer and it is not important how the ally obtains the work. The NLRB has stated that if a customer arranges for substitute service during a strike, neither the customer nor the substitute enterprise can be considered an ally of the struck employer even if the customer knowingly arranges for the services and the substitute knowingly performs them.

7.   Sympathy Strikes.

A "sympathy" strike is a concerted refusal by employees of one bargaining unit to cross a picket line established by a group of employees who are members of a different bargaining unit. A "sympathy" strike often occurs when there is more than one union functioning at an employer's plant. Usually, a more powerful or influential unit will aid another in its walkout for the purpose of union solidarity in support of the workers' demands. The effect on an employer can be staggering, since he may be able to do without the services of the primary strikers but is dependent upon the continued labors of the sympathy strikers.

The National Labor Relations Board and the Courts have recognized the protected, concerted rights of employees to honor picket lines not established by their own union or in their own bargaining unit. The general rule holds that the sympathy striker stands in the shoes of the primary or original striker. This rule is not, however, hard and fast, and the facts of any particular strike situation are more likely to be determinative of the status of the strike than any rule of law. A key issue in determining the rights of employees to engage in sympathy strikes is whether their contract contains a no-strike clause. "No-strike" clauses do not forbid sympathy strikes unless sympathy strikes are specifically included in the prohibition. However, in a relatively recent split decision, the NLRB held that an employer was guilty of violating the Act when it discharged 126 employees who struck in the face of a "no-strike" clause. The Board majority did not view the no-strike pledge as constituting a "clear and unequivocal waiver" of the right to strike against third parties' conduct which affects terms and conditions of employment. The Court of Appeals denied enforcement of the Board's decision and held that the no-strike clause at issue was drafted in such a manner as to constitute a waiver by the union of its right to strike over otherwise nonarbitrable disputes. Normally if the right to engage in a sympathy strike is not specifically forbidden by the no-strike clause, employees may engage in a sympathy strike and honor the picket line. Furthermore, these strikers, even though governed by a general "no-strike" clause, would be in the same legal position as the primary strikers. It should be evident, therefore, that an employer must insist at the bargaining table on inclusion of a prohibition of sympathy strikes in the no-strike clause. There are also numerous cases that stand for the proposition that a contract should include a separate, all inclusive, no-strike clause and a no-strike clause in conjunction with the grievance arbitration

clause. This will help protect the company against
employee strikes over non-arbitrable issues.

   8. Partial Strikes.

One of the most recently employed tactics of unions
involves the use of the partial or intermittent strike.
Under this type of job action employees, individually or as
a complete bargaining unit, stop working for short but critical periods of time to disrupt overall operations. After
the employer has made the necessary adjustments to cover
the apparent strike, the employees return to work. Another
more conventional form of a partial strike is the "blue
flu". Under this arrangement, certain members of the bargaining unit call in sick with the result being disruption
of the department, particularly when large numbers of unanticipated sicknesses occur. This type of work stoppage,
though effective at times, poses some distinctively different problems for both management and the union. First,
these strikes are harder to control by the union because
the behavior requested of the employees is more complex
than that involved in total strikes. The degree of dis-
obedience to the employer is more ambiguous and immediate.
Therefore, traditional labor sympathies/alliances are not

as easily invoked. Additionally, partial strikes generally put less pressure than total strikes on an employer to reach agreements because most of the work is in fact being done. Partial strikes can cause irrevocable damage to the labor/management relationship. Management must cope with the daily disruption caused by this absenteeism. This can be particularly trying if the absenteeism affects critical points in the work process or if a product deadline looms near.

This type of employee economic activity is not regulated by the states or the NLRB. The NLRA does not consider these economic devices to be unlawful. Similarly, these brief, unannounced walkouts are generally not protected by state law and a state employment board cannot order a union to cease interfering with production by promoting or calling sudden and intermittent union meetings or temporary work stoppages during regular working hours. Congress clearly meant to leave the use of such tactics unregulated. However, where employees engage in such unregulated economic warfare, the employer may wish to counter with economic weapons such as a lockout, hiring of replacements or appropriate discipline.

9. Replacement Workers.

Replacement workers are those employees hired by an employer as replacements for striking bargaining unit members. The statute granting the right of employees to strike does not deny an employer the right to protect and continue his business by filling the jobs left vacant by strikers. Therefore, when strikers resort to various forms of work stoppages, the employer is entitled to respond with efforts to preserve production and he must have latitude in hiring replacement workers. Basically, the exercise of this option involves a management decision to hire either "temporary" or "permanent" replacements through the local labor market. Employers must be extremely careful as to the conditions under which replacements are hired - i.e., temporary or permanent. It is probably safest for an employer to call these new workers "replacements" because at the time of their hiring it is often uncertain as to whether it is an economic or unfair labor practice strike.

C. Analysis of the Strike Setting.

The initial questions to be asked by an employer in preparing for a potential strike should center on an analysis of the employee unit:

-- What is the age distribution of the people in the unit?

-- What is the proportion of men to women in the unit?

-- Is the unit composed of strong labor-oriented people?

-- Does the unit operate democratically or does it follow the dictates of a few leaders?

-- How militant has this union been in the past?

Answers to these questions will dictate some definite planning priorities. For instance, it is presumed that women are less likely to cause violence on the picket line and that older employees and/or heads of families are less likely to want a strike.

Secondly, the employer must assess the financial position (stability) of the union:

Can the union afford a strike?

Will the international union support the strike?

If so, to what extent?

What is the size of the union treasury?

What is the current membership of the union?

Has the union decreased in size?

Has the union recently cut back on its internal staffing?

Another area of concern is union leadership:

Does the union leadership have control over its members or is there open opposition to their leaders?

Do the union leaders have their members prepared mentally, economically, and emotionally to strike?

Does the union present a united front?

Do the strike issues affect a majority of the bargaining unit?

Do the strike issues affect the union leaders personally?

It is important to ascertain whether the employees are organized enough to strike and whether the employees have the personal and economic inclination to strike. Management's strike plan is a strategic response to threatened strike activity. In this way, it is a defensive plan and must be prepared to meet the pressures and circumstances brought about by the individual union. Management's response must also take into account the company's own unique position. Accordingly, management must analyze the company's vulnerability to a strike. Whether management is able to take a strike is a critical decision. The risk in negotiations depends on what one is likely to lose in the event of a strike. This analysis is central to the threshold management decision as to whether or not the company can afford to take a strike.

Once the decision is made to take a strike, there is no turning back. If the company is going to capitulate to union demands, it is best to do it before a strike begins. If the company caves in at some subsequent date, it may serve as a long-lasting reminder to the employees that when the going gets tough, the company bails out. This leaves the impression that the employees need only threaten to strike the next time around to maximize bargaining leverage in negotiations.

Once the strike begins, the employer is compelled to preserve management's integrity and maintain a respectable bargaining position for the future. The settlement problem arises from the fact that the union faces the exact same dilemma. Usually a strike need not mean closing down the company. The task then is to evaluate the company's position and to devise a plan for the company to minimize the strike's effect and continue its operations.

D. <u>Effective Strike Prevention</u>.

1. <u>Use of the Mediator</u>.

The use of state or federal mediation services can effectively reduce the likelihood of an actual strike.

Although mediation is a voluntary process, it can be advantageous to have the services of a mediator available if the negotiations are approaching an impasse. However, a stumbling block in the use of these services arises when either management or the union perceives the request as weakening the party's respective bargaining position. However, the mediator can make it appear that the parties did not ask for the services but rather that the mediator is coming in of his own volition. The mediation agency has already been informed of the dispute based on FMCS Form F-7. Pursuant to Section 8(d) of the NLRA, the employer must notify the union of termination of the existing contract (see Appendix C).

Even if union negotiators feel that the employer's position is the more equitable, they are often reluctant to agree because of their members' reaction. The mediator, sensing the situation, can propose a solution. Since the mediator is making the proposed settlement, the union negotiators can accept the proposal with less trepidation that charges of "sellout" will be directed at them.

Essentially, a mediator will initially confer separately with each party in order to understand the dispute, the progress to date and the roadblocks to an agreement.

If the deadlock has resulted from a misunderstanding, the mediator will try to correct it in a joint or separate conference. If there is a personality conflict or lack of sufficient authority, the mediator might suggest a change in negotiators or subsequent increase in their authority. The mediator may schedule a joint session and help the bargaining parties substitute reason and logic for emotion. He may then hold separate conferences to explore all the issues raised in the joint meeting while suggesting compromises or alternative approaches. Finally, a mediator will remind the deadlocked parties of their obligations to the public and the long-term ramifications of a strike. In this regard, a mediator may effectively prevent a strike situation by bringing indirect pressure on the parties in his capacity as a representative of the public.

2. Saving Room for Movement.

For some employers, winning at the bargaining table means hammering the union into submission. For others, it entails settling on almost any terms, as long as a strike is averted. For most companies, winning involves a mutually satisfactory settlement between these two extremes. However, it should always mean negotiating an agreement that comes close to achieving pre-established bargaining goals. A realistic, well-defined set of bargaining objectives is a necessity for all employers.

Ideally, bargaining goals should be grouped into three categories. First are those goals that represent the optimum, realistic desires of the employer, that is, those that seem out of reach but which just might be attainable, short of a strike, if the employer's power evaluation is accurate. Another category consists of bargaining goals that are likely to be achieved in a skillfully negotiated compromise settlement. Lastly, there are those goals representing the maximum concessions the employer must obtain before taking a strike or imposing a lockout.

Realistic bargaining goals will reflect a basic, long-range labor relations plan as well as immediate contingencies. A clearly defined policy provides the company's negotiator with a knowledgeable frame of reference for bargaining. However, the negotiator should always be prepared to shift position a bit even if it means returning to top management to get more authority. By saving room for movement during negotiations, the company will not put the union in the position of having its "back to the wall". This tactic may force the union to call a strike just to save face with its own membership. Accordingly, the ability to "give and take" during bargaining may very well be the key to effective strike prevention.

3. Maintaining Leverage in Bargaining by Continued Operations.

The ability of management to maintain leverage in bargaining is crucial to effective strike prevention. The ability to take a strike rather than submit to union demands is the employer's most potent weapon in collective bargaining. The decision and commitment to operate during the strike may act as a deterrent to strike activity. The willingness to take a strike should reduce the advantages likely to be gained by the union through strike action. Accordingly, the initial effect of continued operation should force a reappraisal by the union of its likelihood of prevailing. The result may be an enhanced willingness on the union's part to seek and accept a compromise on key strike issues. The long range effect of the employer's commitment to operate should enhance the credibility of its threat to take a long strike, resulting in more moderate settlements with fewer strikes. Accordingly, management can use its ability to continue operations to gain and maintain leverage in bargaining. As a result, any union threat to walk out and paralyze the company cannot be effectively used to "hold over management's head."

4.   Timing of the Strike (Product and Contract Duration).

Generally, the type of product produced by the company will be a consideration as to when the union will call a strike. For example, the union may have its members walk off the line during the period when perishable goods must be immediately processed. Additionally, if the company is under contract to produce a special order, the union may wish to strike prior to processing the order.

An example of timing the strike to take advantage of a company's vulnerability recently occurred at a meat processing plant. The exact hour of the strike was pinpointed by determining the most critical time in the plant's operations. As soon as all of the carcasses were moved out of the cooler and sliced, the employees walked off. The meat would be ruined if not immediately processed. However, assessing the timing of the strike before it occurred allowed management to plan well in advance as to how to continue the operations.

The duration of the contract itself is an important consideration in strike prevention. If, at the expiration of the present contract, the state of the economy is in a downswing, the union membership may not be as willing to strike. Also, tying a union down to a longer contract may lessen the opportunities for strike action. Most northern employers prefer to have contracts expire in the winter in order to deter picketing and/or strikes due to the cold weather. If the union is aware of these precautionary steps, it may help to deter a strike.

5.   Creativity in Bargaining.

Creative bargaining can be effectively used throughout negotiations. The countless bargaining techniques can be constructively designed or modified to keep the negotiations moving forward thereby lessening the likelihood of a strike.

Some specific techniques for bargaining include the use of continuous bargaining around the clock. Also, if the employer feels there may be a crisis impending, a mediator could be brought in from the beginning and continue in the deliberations until settlement. The mediator could also be held in the background and be used on an "as needed" basis.

The company could also bring in key, high level executives on a select basis to resolve complex issues. Further, in the discussion of a contract, the parties could decide that the non-economic aspects will be negotiated individually, and if not resolved, they could be submitted to arbitration. Management may also choose to bargain through the media by explaining their position. (See Appendix D for a sample advertisement.) Also, in order to stimulate early ratification, the parties may agree (or the employer may decide) that the contract will not have retroactivity. Management could also announce its plans for implementation of its final offer. This encourages early action because if the union ratifies much later, the contract is retroactive only to the date of ratification. Conversely, in order to encourage early agreement, there is a technique referred to as pre-activity. When a point of dispute between management and union is agreed upon, the new term goes into effect on the date of that ratification. Another bargaining technique involves the proposal of a multi-year contract with limited wage reopeners. Although the wages may be reconsidered during the life of the contract, many of the side issues that would cause problems between the parties are eliminated. For example, if plant relocation becomes a perceived problem, it could be eliminated as an issue by agreeing to reopen on that issue.

The negotiator should try to keep the sessions moving smoothly by proposing new alternatives to old methods of bargaining. The techniques described above, though not inclusive, may revive stagnant negotiations, thereby preventing an impending strike. The concepts are stated generally and it is essential that the bargaining options be explored based on local conditions.

III. STRUCTURING THE MANAGEMENT STRIKE TEAM

A. Formation of the Management Strike Team.

The essential elements of a successful strike plan are structural and organizational. It is imperative that certain individuals be responsible for specific, well-defined tasks during the strike. These individuals who are assigned to the strike management team will coordinate plant activities during the strike, maintain plant security, coordinate legal activities and plan defensive actions to meet the threats of union sabotage and violence. The precise duties and the number of people assigned to undertake them will vary depending upon the size of the operation, the nature of the strike, staffing abilities, and the physical plant in which the company functions. This analysis may be easily adapted to meet the needs and concerns of an individual company but certainly each of these areas should be assigned to a specific member of the strike team.

The strike team should be established well in advance of any strike. As soon as the legitimate rumors of a strike surface, management must move into action. Often the first move to make when a strike appears imminent is to contact legal counsel and apprise him of the overall situation. This way the company's exposure is minimized relative to legal consequences. Legal counsel should also be able to realistically advise management as to the potential issues of an unfair labor practice strike. The action that a company takes at this point will be more credible to management and the employees when based on initial reliance on legal counsel. Threshold decisions as to continued operations, settlement possibilities, continued bargaining and decertification may be made with more confidence with expert legal advice. It is always advisable to seek counsel _before_ acting rather than to expect an attorney miraculously to hold management harmless after the mistakes have already been made. Once contact has been made with an attorney, the next move is to assemble the management strike team. What follows is a general analysis of each member of the management strike team followed immediately by a more detailed checklist of each member's respective duties.

B. Responsibilities Before and During Strike.

1. Responsibilities of the Strike Coordinator.

The fundamental responsibility of the management strike team during the strike is to plan strategy and coordinate all activities. These duties are to be handled by the strike coordinator. A likely candidate for this position is the head of the industrial relations department or perhaps even the president of the company. The key is to have someone in this position with authority, someone who is well respected and able to make firm and prompt decisions. In strike situations, decisions have to be made on the spot and there is no time for procrastination.

One of the main responsibilities of the strike coordinator is to keep his team under complete control. It is important that the management team remain in control and level-headed when tension mounts. As an example of what can happen, consider the following scenario:

The strike is a few weeks old and management is putting in long hard hours. The strikers are getting weary as well, and are upset at the lack of progress in negotiations. There is tension and even open hostility. One morning a supervisor tries to drive into work and several pickets walking in front of the entrance bend over to tie their shoes. Several minutes elapse without the pickets' moving. Meanwhile, threats are shouted at the driver and menacing movements are made. The supervisor gets upset and hits the accelerator. He then leaves his car and gets into a fist fight with the strikers.

The problems posed by this very typical incident demonstrate the need for everyone to understand their role, be aware of the proper actions required by the circumstances, and to keep matters in proper perspective. The strike will end eventually and a high priority must be placed on minimizing the scars that remain. Certainly, physical injuries to people involved on one side or another will only widen the gap between the parties. Furthermore, a calming influence by management will diffuse some of the union's emotional spirit and support. If management allows picket line activities to openly frustrate and disturb them, management will reinforce picket line activities aimed at disrupting operations. The bottom line is that the strike coordinator must control the overall situation by a

-33-

realistic explanation to everyone involved as to the ultimate goals of the management team and the need to act calmly and intelligently throughout the crisis.

Another major task of the strike coordinator is to implement the strike plan and direct activities from the strike headquarters. The headquarters may be, depending on the militancy of the situation, either on or off the company premises. Obviously, there is a certain convenience of maintaining regular operations by locating strike headquarters within the plant. However, there may be advantages to having the strike headquarters located elsewhere. Pickets will attempt to record all of management's activities. This includes listing the names or license numbers of people coming to work. These people and their families can be harassed at their homes. It is not unusual for a spouse or children to apply pressure upon a member of management to settle a strike for personal rather than economic reasons. Another harassment technique derived from this type of situation is for strikers to tailgate employees home from the plant. Furthermore, even without this sort of harassment, the strikers will make it difficult for non-striking employees and visitors to pass through the picket line. It is a good idea to minimize the likelihood of contact between the parties as much as possible. Naturally, all aspects of the management strike team and its planning should be kept highly confidential. If the location of a strike headquarters off the premises was leaked to the union, it could be harmful to management.

Additionally, the strike coordinator should establish an unlisted phone line at the headquarters. Strikers may attempt to jam the company's phone lines with calls during a strike to frustrate business. An unlisted phone number may be given to customers and the phone should be available for outgoing calls. This is a good idea no matter where the strike headquarters is located.

The strike coordinator should also coordinate all legal matters with legal counsel. These matters include concerns over injunctions, replacement workers, violence on the picket line, and bargaining procedures. The following is a listing of the responsibilities of the Strike Coordinator:

Strike Coordinator Checklist:

a. Overall responsibility for coordination of the Management Strike Team.

b. Coordination with legal counsel on all matters with legal ramifications including disciplinary matters relating to the strike, unfair labor practice charges with NLRB as well as injunctions sought in state and federal district courts. (See Appendix E, Disciplinary Notice)

c. Orientation of supervisors.

    i. Instruct as to the employer's legal rights.

    ii. Instruct as to strikers' legal rights.

    iii. Advise supervisors of the legal rights of nonstrikers.

    iv. Advise supervisors to avoid arguments or conflicts which would promote dissension.

    v. Orient supervisors on the issues and _update them frequently_.

    vi. Instruction/supervision as to the laws of evidence for proof of unlawful activity.

    vii. Maintain and enforce confidentiality amongst all employees.

    viii. Keep everyone as calm as possible. The union wants to provoke an incident. Police will help but everyone must be _patient_.

2. _Responsibilities of Security Coordinator_.

The security coordinator is in charge of security for the plant and all employees working at the plant during the strike. The first task for the coordinator should be to personally talk to the police before the strike begins and

-36-

inform them of what is likely to occur and what he expects of the police department.

If violence breaks out, the security coordinator must decide to contact the police. The security coordinator also helps evaluate arrests and whether strikers should be prosecuted. He also has the duty to safeguard the plant and all company property. Secured entrances, secured perimeters and security guards are essential steps in securing the property.

The security coordinator should coordinate the transportation of the employees to work and secure their entry into the plant. An employee could come to work, lose his temper and overreact to pickets at the plant entrance if he is alone in his car. Furthermore, the reduction in the number of cars minimizes the number of opportunities for problems upon entering the gates and/or vandalism to cars. It is sometimes advantageous to use vans or buses to transport management and replacement workers. The use of buses is not only effective as a practical transportation tool but also can intimidate the strikers on the picket line.

Another area of concern for the security coordinator is the prevention of sabotage by striking employees. This is a difficult assignment. First, he must be prepared for the exact instance in which the strike is going to occur. Strike sabotage usually occurs right at the outset of the strike, especially when the employees are leaving the plant. Some examples of sabotage which strikers have engaged in under such circumstances are: shutting off equipment or putting it in a locked position, removal of essential working parts from equipment, taking/hiding keys as a way to gain access to the plant, destroying inventory information and customer lists, and perhaps even direct damage to plant and equipment. The key to control in this area is to be alert and to organize all managers to implement the management strike plan once the strike occurs.

The security coordinator should also contact the fire department and point out any dangers at or near the plant which could arise during the strike. It is advisable to ensure that the fire department has a floor plan of the company including a floor plan of all entrances and exits during the strike. If there is a fire during the strike, the fire department must have immediate access to the property.

It is also a good idea during the strike to restrict entry to the plant to those who have proper identification.

Planning for this can also begin before the strike. All doors should be locked except for those where guards are posted. Badges may be issued to admissible personnel and instructions given that nobody enters the building without a badge. Strikers should not be invited into the plant during the strike, except to execute the new contract.

The security coordinator must also establish a system to collect all company property before the employees actually leave the premises. This is essential if the employees are to be kept out of the company during the strike. Uniforms, tools, and keys must all be checked at the door before the employees are permitted to leave. The fact that management retains this property gives the employees no legitimate reason to return. These steps assure security and bring permanency to the strike setting. Paychecks should be distributed on the last day before a strike or else mailed to the employees. All of these measures are precautions against sabotage. In addition, management protects itself from fueling the strike by disclosing problems inherent in continued operations. Employees who come in during the strike will look for problems and these failures will inevitably appear in the union newsletter as propoganda fueling their strike. The following checklist summarizes the responsibilities of the security coordinator.

Security Coordinator Checklist:

Pre-Strike

1. Contact local law enforcement authorities before the strike. He may want to make it a joint meeting with the union in order to set ground rules and eliminate the propensity for violence. Explain the number of employees involved, number of gates and the possibility of violence.

    a. Notify the police department, sheriff's department and the mayor where appropriate so that police protection may be furnished.

    b. The police or sheriff's department may limit employee entry to the fewest possible number of entrances.

    c. Leave the names and phone numbers of management personnel who should be contacted in the event of an emergency.

    d. Brief police on picketing guidelines. Prepare handout to be given to pickets (see Appendices F and G, Picket Guidelines and Police Guidelines).

2. If necessary, hire security guards prior to the strike for protection prior to and during the strike. This will help avoid sabotage during the time period immediately preceding the strike.

3. If necessary, hire security guards to ensure the safety of the management team, their families and homes.

4. Arrange car pools and/or vans for all employees working during the strike (including replacements).

5. Take whatever precautionary steps are possible to avoid sabotage prior to the strike. For example, lock desks and doors, carefully monitor use of equipment to avoid breakage or lost parts, be sensitive to critical parts of your operation including: filing systems (missing keys), planning books and operational or repair manuals. It may be necessary to assign security and/or additional supervision to help monitor this area, especially if operating more than one shift.

6. Document all contacts with local law enforcement authorities. <u>Failure of local authorities to take steps to contain violence may be a basis for NLRB intervention to enjoin any violence</u>.

7. Plan for plant maintenance during strike, including such functions as heating, fire protection and protection against property damage.

    a. The fire department should be contacted and a clear understanding should exist as to where changes relating to plant fire protection should be reported.

    b. The fire department should be notified of any changes in locations to which they should respond in the event a fire alarm is received from the plant. It may be possible that some entrances will have been closed, parking lot gates locked, and other temporary arrangements made which will necessitate fire department response at points other than where set up for normal plant operation. If the fire department has been furnished with the plant layout showing points of response, it may be advisable to furnish them with a revised layout.

c. The fire department should be promptly notified of any important changes in fire protection facilities in a plant. This would include shutting off sprinkler systems; presence of new or exceptional hazards in or near the plant, including the building of bonfires, erection of tents or shanties which may not conform with the building codes; the presence of few employees in the plant who are available for fighting fires should they occur; and any other factors which may be detrimental to adequate fire protection.

d. Precautions should be taken to remove or reduce hazards which might cause fire. This would include the cleaning of equipment; safe storage of paints, lacquers, thinners, gasoline and other inflammable materials; proper storage of oxygen and acetylene; removal of oily rags or other refuse; and other fire prevention precautions. Persons assigned to protect the plants should continue these precautions so that no fire may be caused by neglect.

e. Consideration should be given to formulating a policy that the fire department be called for all plant fires. Plant policy may be that the fire department should only be called in the event a fire is out of control or is likely to get out of control. Reconsideration of this latter practice is advisable, at least for the duration of a labor dispute.

f. Leave the names and home phone numbers of management personnel who should be contacted in the event of an emergency.

8. Establish identification badges to be distributed to nonstriking employees once the strike is commenced.

9. Stress the critical importance of proper identification of persons entering the employer's facilities and which gates they enter.

10. In some strikes, strikers have permitted plant protection personnel, power house workers and certain maintenance workers to enter the plant. Striking unionists have, in the past, offered admittance to payroll department employees in the hope that paychecks for strikers will be delivered on payday. In such an event, payroll employees should not enter the plant as long as entrance is denied other office or supervisory personnel.

11. Arrange for collection from employees going on strike of <u>all</u> employer equipment (tools, keys, uniforms, etc.).

12. Designate a management headquarters.

    a. Consideration should be given to the eventual necessity of establishing a temporary management headquarters outside the plant for carrying on necessary employer business. This would require necessary employer records, telephone facilities, typewriters, employer stationery and supplies sufficient to carry on necessary communications with suppliers, customers and employees.

    b. In the event of a strike blockade of multiple plant locations, arrangements should be made in advance as to where the manager, personnel director or other designated key officials may be reached by telephone.

    c. It is advisable to keep the plant switchboard and teletype equipment open if possible. Consideration should be given to keeping sufficiently trained, trusted personnel in the plant for this purpose. There may be repeated attempts to jam the phone lines. If so, utilize unlisted phone numbers.

d. Plant protection should see that any received messages which may be undelivered are taken to a point which should be designated. Prior arrangements should be made covering this point.

e. Take precautions to restrict the use of phones to necessary employer use only.

During Strike

13. Plant security and operation during strike periods:

a. Plant protection must be <u>visible</u> and constant. Prepare to extend protection by private security force to top officials' homes if necessary. Such person should not become involved in any matter which may unnecessarily tend to aggravate conditions. They should keep a cool head, be firm but courteous, avoid unnecessary conversation relative to the dispute and perform the required duties in an unprovocative way.

b. Preparations should be made for members of supervision to take care of any equipment which may be left unattended by striking hourly employees before supervisors leave the plant.

c. Develop a list of control valves, switches, control centers, alarm boxes, communication equipment, and other critical installations for use by security personnel.

d. Close and lock all unused doors and gates. Change locks at edge-of-premises doors and gates, or by other precautions prevent their being opened without authority. Have duplicate keys available at strike headquarters.

e. Close and lock all first floor outside windows which may be exposed to streets or other open areas.

f. Arrange standby service with: locksmith (to change locks), plumbing, garage and window repair services. Have a list of names and phone numbers of persons prepared to cross picket lines to perform these services.

g. Start and continue regular hourly patrols of buildings which have few or no employees in them.

h. Give close attention to employee cars in parking lots.

i. Receive and record any complaints made by employees -- interference, damage to their property, etc.

j. Unless instructions are received to the contrary, see that regularly used employee entrances are opened at shift starting times so that there may be no charges of lockout.

k. Plant protection personnel should make daily inspections of perimeter fences and coordinate with the managing officer when gaps or breaks in the fence are discovered.

l. Due to the fact that a union could represent your employees as well as the employees of the law enforcement agencies who are charged with the protection

-45-

of your employees and property, be especially alert to the type and quality of their services.

3. <u>Responsibilities of Striker/Fringe Benefit</u> <u>Coordinator</u>.

The director of strikers' fringe benefits is responsible for the dissemination of the employees' last paycheck and will answer all questions regarding leaves of absence, sick leaves, vacations, and holiday pay. This person should probably be a supervisor from the payroll or bookkeeping department. Certainly, the individual should have some background or experience in employee paychecks, check stubs, and deductions.

The initial task of this coordinator is to distribute the final paychecks. As mentioned earlier, in order to keep the employees off the company premises, it is advisable to mail the last paychecks by certified mail to the employees' homes.

This coordinator must also handle all of the questions which arise regarding the continuation of employee benefits during the strike. Usually these questions must be handled on a case-by-case basis. You cannot assume that everybody who fails to show up for work is necessarily on strike.

There is a responsibility to check a doctor's certification for sick leave and to determine whether the employee is on vacation.

Another issue concerns the payment of insurance benefits during the strike. This is a somewhat more troublesome issue, perhaps best illustrated by the following example:

> An employee has been with a company for twenty years, and that company is paying 100% of his health insurance policy premiums. The union calls a strike. The strike lasts only a month and there is no militancy. In the second week of the strike, the employee's wife was seriously injured and hospitalized. Is it a wise decision for the company to have stopped paying the health insurance premiums when the strike started?

The problem here is more humanitarian than legal. In a strike situation, one must ask, what is to be gained by cutting off insurance benefits? When is this action to be taken and at what potential risk? Long-lasting scars can arise from such a decision. Remember that one of management's goals may be to limit the effects of the strike. Nonetheless, management does have the right to terminate the insurance for which it is paying benefits. Premium payments should be continued to an employee who is on a legitimate leave during the strike. The general rule is that pension and profit sharing benefits do not accrue when the employee is on strike, much the same as seniority does not accrue in this situation. Benefits for employees who are not on strike are maintained at pre-strike levels.

Management definitely does not want to be financing the strike. If the strike occurs during the term of the contract, dues check-off should be eliminated immediately. When the employees are on strike, the union is not honoring the terms of the collective bargaining agreement. To continue dues deduction from those who may not be participating in the strike adds both moral and economic support to the strike. Any wages earned in a strike should be given to the employees directly and not to the union. If the contract has expired, dues check-off and union security obligations expire with it. In the absence of a contract an employer should not make contributions of this kind to a union. The following summarizes the responsibilities of the fringe benefit coordinator.

<u>Strike/Fringe Benefit Coordinator Checklist</u>:

1. Review personnel policies and collective bargaining agreements to ascertain:

   a. Leave of absence rules.

   b. Continuation of group life and health insurance benefits.

    c.   Interruption and accruing credit for purposes of retirement, paid leaves such as vacation and sick leave, time in grade for purposes of probationary period, promotion and seniority in general. Review holiday pay provisions (you may be required to work the day before and after a holiday) in the event one should occur during a strike.

    d.   Review notice and eligibility requirements for vacation and sick leave. Strikers may apply for these leaves at the onset of a strike.

    e.   Treatment of striking employees who are on authorized leave when the strike begins or are scheduled to commence during strike, or who become sick during the time of the strike.

    f.   Review job specifications to make sure that all duties are covered (in the event of slow-down actions).

2. Accelerate payroll to pay all striking employees their accrued compensation as soon as possible.

3. Remove a supply of disbursement checks from the plant premises.

4. Remove salary records, checks, envelopes and other supplies necessary to mail paychecks to salaried employees to a safe place outside the plant.

5. Mail paychecks to strikers.

6. If necessary, set a limited time and provide supervision for strikers to clean out their lockers.

7. Responsible for making sure there was no dues checkoff or deduction after the expiration of the contract. It is possible for the parties to agree to continue dues deduction after the expiration of the contract.

4.   Responsibilities of the Communications Coordinator.

The communications coordinator is likely to be someone from the public relations department or upper management. His or her first responsibility is to prepare an updated list of employees' home addresses and spouses' names, and to coordinate all contacts with all of them through the mail.   It may be advisable to address all communications to the spouse in order to make this a family decision. Communicating with the employees is important for several reasons; it balances the propaganda being fed to them by the union, it may enhance the possibility for settlement, and it demonstrates a continuation of management's concern in maintaining an open and healthy employment relationship.

The law allows some contact with striking employees. An employer may inform the striking employees of his last offer and make that same offer to any returning employees.   However, an employer may not offer returning employees greater wages or benefits than those embodied in his last offer to the union.   It is a good idea to make all employees aware of final offers and to highlight in a letter what has been accomplished in negotiations.   The communication should describe and explain the company's bargaining position. Many unions distort the reports of bargaining sessions in order to keep the fire fueled and encourage support, enthusiasm and unity for the strike.

The communications coordinator should also contact all suppliers and customers of the company to inform them of the strike and the possibility of a picket line. Will the suppliers cross the picket line? If not, new suppliers must be found whenever possible. The communications coordinator must work with the strike coordinator to coordinate new company phone numbers and to devise a phone system that is insulated from union attempts to jam the phone lines with calls.

The communications coordinator also has the duty to make media contacts and to handle all press releases. It is a mistake to have more than one company spokesman during the strike. The correct story with facts must be presented to the press on a day-to-day basis. Complete accuracy is of paramount importance. Hopefully, the communications coordinator will have established prior contacts in the media who can be counted on and utilized to present a fair and unbiased version of the strike. The press should be notified of events as they happen and kept current on all progressing negotiations. The reporting of any picket line misconduct is especially important. Management has a greater duty than the union to report to the press because the company needs to prevent distortions and to responsibly inform the public of its positions. Adverse publicity from a strike can have long-term repercussions, not only in the local community but with customers as well.

Another duty of this person is to serve as company spokesman to gather community support. A well orchestrated campaign by the company may also result in mounting public support for a settlement. Frequently companies with attractive wage and benefit packages place full or half page ads outlining pertinent facts to the community (See Appendix D). This type of communication can be particularly effective where adverse reaction to a strike can cause a company to lose a significant share of their market to competitors. In addition, elected officials and community interest groups should be contacted and informed as to the strike issues as well as management's position regarding the strike.

The following checklist outlines pertinent concerns for the communications coordinator.

Communications Coordinator Checklist:

1. Set up a method of contact with entire supervisory staff to keep this group informed on strike developments. Organization of all staff meetings during strike (you may want to set a regular meeting time).

2. Update the list of all supervisory personnel with home addresses and telephone numbers; maintain that list outside the plant.

3. Prepare a complete list of employees, hourly and salaried, including home addresses, spouses' names and phone numbers. Keep that complete list outside the plant.

4. Prepare two sets of envelopes addressed to hourly and salaried employees and remove to outside the plant for possible use in communicating with employees. Separate envelopes of striking employees from nonstriking employees based on payroll records.

5. Prepare specific and individual plans to inform vendors, customers, sales force, transportation officials, and stockholders in the event a strike takes place.

6. Special unlisted telephone lines to key locations and officials. Use of two-way radios.

7. Use of standby courier service.

8. Maintain emergency telephone list of key officials.

9. Special phone line to notify nonstriking employees where and when to report to work.

10. Sole responsibility for all media contacts including TV, radio and newspaper interviews (employer spokesperson).

11. Responsible for all press releases including possible ads for strike replacements (take initiative whenever possible).

12. Responsible for maintaining an up-to-date mailing list for all press releases.

13. Coordinate unlisted phone numbers for work and key management people at their homes.

14. Coordinate all mass mailings to strikers and/or employees (you may want to prepare labels in advance). Contents of all letters and press releases should be reviewed by legal counsel.

15. Arrange to pick up mail at the Post Office. Postal workers will not cross the picket lines.

16. Responsible for regular newsletters.

17. Represent employer at local meetings (appear before Lions Club, Kiwanis, Rotary, city council, etc.).

18. Communicate the message that the employer is ready and willing to negotiate and to try to reach agreement at any time.

19. Keep negotiation sessions <u>closed</u> to the media.

20. Do not attack personalities but rather the validity of the union's position.

5. <u>Responsibilities of the Picket Line Monitor.</u>

The job of the picket line monitor is likely to be the toughest. His task is to observe what is going on at the gate in order to record and establish any unfair labor practices by the union. The person in this position must be a manager or a supervisory employee who is familiar with the identity of all or most of the employees. He must be able to identify each and every one of the employees to effectively monitor the picket line. It is also helpful if he can recognize the officials, stewards, and international representatives of the union. If not, someone must be readily available to aid him in these tasks.

The picket line monitor must maintain a daily picket log of events that indicate the date, time, number and names of all pickets. He also records on preprinted forms how many picket signs are present and the exact language printed on each sign (see Appendix I). This is important because identifying the content of the signs as well as the object of the picketing may result in an unfair labor practice against the union. In addition to the log, the monitor must record all picket line misconduct. A prepared form should be available to serve as an incident report of any picket line misconduct (see Appendix J).

Picket line misconduct takes many forms. Some examples of misconduct include nails or glass at the entrance, scratched cars, smashed windshields, broken antennas, physical assaults, and profanities. Isolated incidents of these actions may not be unfair labor practices, but the composite repetition of these acts, when viewed in the totality of the circumstances, could result in a finding by the NLRB that a union has restrained or coerced employees with respect to their right to refrain from strike activity, and in short, may result in a violation of the NLRA. Additionally, the employer may wish to make a request under the Freedom of Information Act for examples of previous union picket line misconduct. (See Appendix H for a sample request.) This information could be used for several purposes by the company. A single incident of a striker swearing at a manager probably would not result in finding the union guilty of an unfair labor practice, yet it may be important in the context of other activities. Individual actions of employees may be dealt with in some fashion outside of filing a charge with the NLRB. Thus an employee who has been assaulted by a striker should fill out an incident form (Appendix J) and then go to the local police authorities. Management may refuse to reinstate that striker after the strike is settled.

Responsibility for pictures of picket line violence also falls to the picket line monitor. This may sound like an easy job, but it is, in fact, quite a sensitive concern. It is illegal to take photographs or motion pictures of picketing unless there is reasonable cause to suspect that violence is going to take place. The rule of law is that one may take pictures to establish picket line misconduct to aid in obtaining an injunction, but may not interfere with the picket line activities in this manner unless there is violence. Photographing pickets may constitute surveillance or may be interpreted as intimidation and violative of Section 8(a)(1) of the NLRA. It is permissible under the NLRA to make a distinction between "casual and normal observation" of strikers as a legal activity. It might involve a written record of strike activities and surveillance, which might be placed on film. The reasoning behind this legal difference is that the camera is viewed as somehow threatening or intimidating to the pickets and, arguably restricts their legal right to picket. However, an observer with a note pad does not interfere with employees' rights as his presence is plainly evident and, therefore, does not constitute surveillance, and involves no coercion or limitation on their freedom to act. One recommendation is to keep a person inside the company with a telephoto lens ready to take pictures at the first outbreak of violence. It is a tremendous advantage to have still pictures (black and white) and/or movies when proving an unfair labor practice charge of picket line misconduct.

Another task to be performed by the picket line monitor is the recording of all vehicles at or near the picket line. The reason for this is that a car could go by and someone might throw something out of the window or harass other vehicles. It is, therefore, important to be cognizant of those walking by the gate and vehicles stopped or driving nearby.

The location of the monitor is also important. There may be a danger in stationing too close to the strikers. That could pose security and safety problems. The observer may have to be inside the building or in his car nearby.

It is also important to pick the right type of a person for this job. He may be harrassed, sworn at and his car may be kicked. Depending on the size of the plant and the difficulty of these duties, perhaps several people will be needed to do this job effectively. These duties are extremely important and all care should be taken in performing them. Remedying picket line misconduct could provide the leverage for settlement, as it definitely enhances the employer's image in the community and creates sympathy for the employer's position. The following is a listing of the responsibilities of the Picket Line Monitor:

Picket Line Monitor Checklist:

1. Maintain and record a current daily picket log (see Appendix I, Picket Log) which indicates a daily detailed record of the employees picketing. (Date, time, place, name of employees, content of picket signs.)

2. Become familiar with all the employees and union officers, agents and/or representatives.

3. Monitor and record all evidence of picket line misconduct (see Appendix J, Incident Report) which indicates the dates, time, place, circumstances and names of all persons who observed the incident. It is of paramount importance to record the names of all union officers and/or agents in order to establish agency responsibility for the conduct of their members.

4. Coordinate use of camera and filming of misconduct on the picket line.

   a. Use black and white film for reproduction (and be sure to use a telephoto lens and maintain a low profile). You can only take pictures if you have reasonable cause to believe there will be problems, otherwise it is unlawful surveillance. Have back-up equipment available. It is possible that strikers could break the camera or it could malfunction.

   b. Document dates and times of photographed incidents of misconduct and start a new roll of film each day if necessary to identify the date of the film later on. Be sure to date each roll of film.

5. Record the license plates of all cars and trucks at or near the picket line, the names of drivers (if known), the make of vehicle, and the time and date of the observation.

6. When and if strike replacements are hired, you should increase the picket line monitors at the start and end of the shifts. Replacements can breed violence.

6. Responsibilities of the Staffing Supervisor.

The person in charge of maintaining operations and running the plant during the strike is the staffing supervisor. His task is critical at the beginning of the strike. A good example of the type of planning and action that this coordinator must manage is provided by a recent newspaper strike. Employees from five unions at the publishers of the two largest newspapers of a midwestern city went out on strike at 2:00 a.m. The presses were all ready to roll when the walkout occurred. Management literally won that strike on the first day because its team was ready and able to step in and publish the newspapers that day. In this situation, there was no time to hire replacement workers. The only solution was organization and hard work. Even if management has to work 24 hours that first day to maintain plant operations, it is well worth it because the initial success could break the strike and secure the position of the company.

Another concern of the staffing supervisor is to identify who will cross the picket line. The employer is legally allowed to ask each employee in advance whether or not they intend to cross the picket line. An employee may refuse to answer, at which point management cannot force a response, but simple questioning is neither interrogation nor surveillance. The purpose of this questioning is to determine staffing needs during the strike. This problem becomes especially acute if the company is subject to sympathy strikes. It is also important to determine if maintenance people, government inspectors and/or refuse collectors will work during the strike. Are continued operations likely to cause a health or safety problem without these people, and can they be replaced?

The staffing supervisor must also determine the critical functions of the operation. What services and goods are absolutely essential to the maintenance of operations? The supervisor must make plans to continue these services and have enough materials for production available. This may entail some stockpiling of the materials used in production prior to the strike.

The staffing supervisor must also hire replacement employees, organize management personnel to work during the strike, and provide for the needs and safety of all people working during the strike. Sometimes live-in accommodations must be set up. There are companies available who will bring in beds and prepare hot meals, and they will cross any picket line to do so. This will minimize picket line contact with the workers and help to defuse the strike while keeping the plant functioning. Other advantages are that this option results in unity among workers and saves transportation time. Arrangements may be made to take these people home two to three nights a week to be with their families. The presence of cots or beds also allows employees to lay down and relax intermittently during the long stretches of work that are required.

Daily staffing reports must be prepared to know who is and who is not actually working (see Appendix K). The need for replacement workers is determined from these reports. The staffing supervisor also should have the right to discipline employees during the strike. The risk of turning an economic strike into an unfair labor practice strike is too great to act imprudently in this area without legal consultation.

Staffing Supervisor Checklist:

1. Adopt policies for non-union personnel and supervisory personnel who continue to work during the strike. Some strikers may cross the picket line as well. Assess the honesty and integrity of the returning strikers.

    a. Determine whether they will continue to work and where.

    b. Make provisions for preparation of payroll.

    c. Determine with Security Coordinator whether special transportation arrangements should be made to bring these personnel into work.

2. Establish by facility, job classification, position, location and shift on a employee wide basis the relative level of essential services provided which must be maintained.

3. Determine an emergency staffing plan:

    a. Plan, position by position, which functions at which facilities must be staffed to maintain varying levels of decreased operations down to the minimum acceptable level.

    b. Determine, position by position, alternate staffing for varying levels of decreased operation (departmental and nondepartmental management, supervisory and other nonrepresented unit personnel) on an individual by individual basis, as well as nonemployee sources.

    c. Develop training to be conducted periodically for substitute employee "task forces."

    d. Arrange for potential private subcontracting (the union can picket the subcontractor), including refuse collection, private security (with security coordinator), emergency maintenance, custodial, etc.

e. Review licenses required for operating essential equipment and vehicles, if applicable, and ensure that adequate licensed personnel will be available among substitute employees.

4. Plan alternative schedules for production work.

5. Plan alternative work sites for production work and delivery of supplies.

6. Evaluate emergency or critical supplies and stockpile essential operating supplies and raw ingredients in alternate sites where processing will occur.

7. Contact suppliers regarding incoming supplies and outgoing deliveries.

    a. An up-to-date list of all suppliers should be removed from the plant proper to the recommended outside temporary management headquarters. In the event of a strike, it would be necessary to contact these concerns to stop or reroute the flow of incoming materials.

    b. Ascertain the need for temporary storage facilities for incoming materials en route in the event access to the plant premises is denied.

8. Make arrangements for live-in facilities for key personnel (food, sanitation and bedding).

9. Arrangements for comfort of nonstriking employees (coffee, radios, food, etc.).

10. Review and maintain "Daily Staffing Reports" submitted by supervisors. (See Appendix K, Daily Staffing Report.)

11. Review and maintain "Daily Withdrawal of Service Reports" submitted by supervisors and coordinate with other key management officials. (See Appendix L, Daily Withdrawal of Service Report.)

12. Determine a tentative timetable for and number of employees hired as strike replacements. Assist in the hiring process of strike replacements.

13. Be prepared for the first day of the strike as it is critical to stay operational and to be organized right from the outset. The chances are that the employees will walk out at the most vulnerable or critical time for the employer.

14. Do not fire, terminate, lay off or discipline <u>any</u> employee without first consulting with legal counsel. You could be set up for an unfair labor practice strike.

15. Check with appropriate and necessary inspectors to see whether they will cross picket lines and make arrangements for them to do so at operating facilities.

B. <u>Strike Instructions to Supervisors</u>.

1. <u>General Instructions on Work During Strike</u>.

As previously noted, supervisors will play an integral part in the success or failure of the employer to withstand a strike. Therefore, the employer should provide all supervisory personnel with a detailed set of instructions regarding their overall role in the employer's strike plan.

The employer should initially stress in its instructions to supervisory personnel that the company is open for business and work as usual. The company is not on strike; only the union is on strike. Therefore, supervisors, office employees and other employees not represented by the union are expected to report for work as usual.

Crossing the picket line is one of the dangers associated with working during a strike. Therefore, the supervisors who cross the picket line should observe the following rules for their own benefit and safety. On entering or leaving company property in an automobile, the supervisor should wait until the pickets have cleared in order to pass through. Workers should not try to force their way through the line by driving the auto into the pickets. Also, the workers should obey all traffic laws and law enforcement officials. A preliminary injunction may be in effect to protect the rights of those who desire to cross the picket line. If the employee has any difficulty in entering or leaving, the employee should report it to the local law enforcement officials and to the employer.

In addition, to keep problems at the picket line to a minimum, the supervisors should not talk with pickets and should not attempt to handle any misconduct on their own. Legally, strikers are not entitled to block or hinder persons seeking to enter or leave the company premises. If any attempt is made to threaten the workers or prevent them from entering or leaving, the worker should report it immediately. Similarly, the employer does not want and would not condone any intimidation or misconduct directed toward any strikers. If such intimidation or misconduct occurs either at the picket line or away from the plant, the supervisor should see to it that it is reported immediately. (See Appendix J, Incident Report.)

2. Conversations with Striking Employees.

Contacts with striking employees should be avoided and kept to a minimum. In particular, the supervisor should not take the initiative in contacting strikers regarding the hiring of replacements or any other matter. The supervisor cannot solicit, induce, threaten or promise any employees special benefits to encourage them to cross the picket line for work. If the supervisor is questioned or contacted by strikers, he or she should write down what was said, either during the conversation or immediately afterwards, and turn in the report. Also, the supervisor is free to explain the employer's contract offer or the employer's position on the union's contract offer. However, the supervisor should not negotiate with any employee, nor should he try to persuade employees that the employer's proposals should be accepted.

If a striker asks what effect the hiring of replacements has on him, under no circumstances should the supervisor tell him he has been discharged, terminated, laid off or fired. Instead, the supervisor should tell the striker that his status as an active employee cannot be determined until he applies for reinstatement to work. If a striker asks about returning to work, the supervisor should tell him that employees who are represented by the union are free to report to work and may refuse to strike and/or engage in picket line activity. These employee rights are protected by federal law. Employees represented by the union who want to strike and picket are privileged to do so under the law. The choice is up to each individual employee. The safest route is to not speak to the strikers except in a formal setting.

3. Processing of All Replacement Applicants.

All applicants should be told at the outset that they are being considered for a position as a result of a labor dispute. The applicants should complete, date and sign their job applications, and their applications should be given immediately to the staffing supervisor. If an applicant is hired, the date the applicant is hired, the position and wage rate for which the applicant is hired, and the date that the applicant is to begin work should be noted on the application itself. Additionally, all applicants should be told that, if hired, they will be hired at the wage rate specified in the employer's final offer to the union. Fringe benefits and other terms of employment will be the same as the employer's final offer or the expired union contract.

4. Processing of Striking Employees Returning Before Settlement.

Some striking employees may seek to return to work before the strike is settled. This could signal a significant breakthrough for the company. The following procedures should be utilized: Upon checking in to work, all returning strikers should be directed to report to the staffing supervisor. If this supervisor is unavailable, the supervisor to whom the striker reports will be responsible for logging in the striker. The returning striker should sign in on a log sheet indicating his name, time and the date of return, former job assignment, and seniority date. (See Appendix M, Return from Strike Information Sheet.)

The returnee should be given a time card only when it has been determined that the employee has not participated in picket line misconduct, and that there is an opening in the employee's former job classification or substantially equivalent job classification. (These returns to work are presumed to be from an economic strike.) Employees normally will be assigned to available jobs in the order in which they return to work, not by seniority. If there are no available job classifications for which a returning employee is qualified, he should be told that he will be sent home and considered available for recall if and when job openings do occur. Further, any employee who indicates he is quitting employment with the employer should be asked to sign a statement to that effect with a management witness present. (See Appendix N, Resignation.)

C. Legal and Practical Considerations During the Strike.

1. The Legal Dilemma.

The employer's legal liability is determined by the status of the strike faced by the company. There is usually no legal liability when confronting an "economic" strike, but liability frequently results from the mishandling of an "unfair labor practice" strike. The union may file an unfair labor practice charge during contract negotiations, thus attempting to change the character of the strike from an "economic" strike to an "unfair labor practice" strike. If an employer's unfair labor practice is the cause of the strike, then the strike is an unfair labor practice strike. Unfair labor practice strikers keep their employee status and are entitled to reinstatement within five (5) days upon their unconditional offer to return to work.

The liability in an unfair labor practice strike arises in the context of back pay. If an employer is found to have committed an unfair labor practice which precipitated the strike, he is usually liable for the amount of the striking employees' wages from the time of the uncon-ditional offer to return to work. There have been recent legal developments in the timing of the backpay liability so this area of the law is uncertain as of this time. If the employer is found to have discharged an employee for union activities, liability for the wages of a discharged employee may also be a concern.

When there are unfair labor practices pending with the NLRB alleging that either a failure to bargain in good faith or a discharge of an employee for union activities has occurred, it is important for management to assess if the charges have merit. The reason for reaching an early decision on this matter is that back pay liability begins to accrue five days after the employees make an unconditional offer to return to work. Litigation involving the unfair labor practice charge may take months or even years. As a result, the company's liability for back pay may encompass a period of well over a year if the unfair labor practice strikers are not reinstated until the time the decision on the unfair labor case is announced. The back pay liability begins to run five days after an unconditional offer to return to work, and continues to run if the employees are not recalled. Obviously, the liability for unfair labor practice strikers who have been replaced by other employees during a strike, and never reinstated, can be considerable, especially if there are a large number of strikers who have been replaced.

2. Use of Striker Replacements.

Hiring replacement workers is an option to consider in addition to the use of supervisors and/or stockpiling to keep the plant functioning during the strike. Of course the type of strike which one encounters will determine whether or not replacements (permanent or temporary) are a logical alternative.

From a legal standpoint, the U.S. Supreme Court has recently rendered a decision which has a significant impact on a permanent replacement's contract rights. Specifically, in Belknap v. Hale,3/ the Court held:

> An employer may refuse to reinstate strikers at the end of an economic strike if the employer has promised its strike replacements "permanent employment, subject only to settlement with its employees' union and to a Board unfair labor practice order."

The full import of this holding cannot be overlooked by the employer. Under Belknap, a replacement worker who has been promised "permanent" employment may have a misrepresentation or breach of contract claim against the employer. Specifically, if the employer has promised to keep the replacements on a permanent basis, terminating the replacements to make way for reinstated strikers could give rise to a breach of contract claim. Therefore, as a practical and legal consideration, an employer may wish to condition his offer to replacements and hence avoid conflicting

_____

3/ 55 U.S.L.W. 5079 (U.S. June 30, 1983).

obligations to strikers and replacements in the event of a settlement or NLRB order providing for reinstatement.

Hiring replacement workers is a serious step and it should be implemented only after extensive thought and calculation as to its ramifications. Replacement workers often signify a notice to all employees as to the finality of the management position on the strike. Management should recognize, however, that if its goal is to quickly settle the contract, then there is really no purpose in hiring replacement workers. In any event, management must enter this situation with their eyes open. When the decision is made to replace strikers, those employees face a propensity for violence which is imminent in many industries. It is possible that violence will occur at the plant site on the first day the replacements arrive at the job site.

Management should plan in advance for the day the strike ends and what it will do with the replacements. A mixed work force composed of strikers and nonstrikers may result in low productivity because of the bitter feelings which will remain in the workplace long after the strike is over.

3.   Stockpiling of Inventory in Anticipation of the Strike.

Some businesses can stockpile products and materials. If it is feasible, the move to stockpile should be initiated well before the termination date of the contract. This stockpiling not only allows the company to survive the strike without loss of market share or disruption for its customers, but also signals to the employees the company's willingness and ability to cope with the strike. However, stockpiling by itself is not nearly enough.

Can the supervisory work force continue to process orders, answer the phones, and get the business done during the strike even if the product is available for sale? Management must not overestimate its business projections or underestimate the output or expectations of supervisory and non-union personnel. This consideration is crucial if the products or raw materials are perishable. Everyone involved must understand the demands of continuing opera-tions during a strike: hard work, long hours, and some-times even threats of physical violence and retaliation. Yet, the success derived from continuing operations in this way can be significant. Certainly the stockpiling and the show of management determination to weather the storm will defuse the union's enthusiasm. The ideal situation allows management to say to the striking employees: "We are prepared for a long strike here with little hope for a favorable settlement. In fact, we're saving money because you're out on strike and we don't have to pay wages. Meanwhile, our business is flourishing."

Some situations have occurred in which the employers actually encourage or invite the strike by hard-line bargaining, knowing full well that the product is stockpiled and operations could continue. Of course if stockpiling is done in preparation for a strike which never occurs, management faces the problem of having accumulated costly inventory.

4. Wages and Fringe Benefits For Strikers

a. Wages -- Type and Timing of Payments.

(1) Wages Due and Owing Strikers.

The NLRB and the courts have followed the principle that an employer need not compensate a striking employee for work not performed. Therefore, an employer may generally withhold wages and benefits in the nature of

-76-

wages from strikers as long as those wages or benefits were not accrued prior to the initiation of the strike.

The clearest example of an accrued benefit is earned wages. Employees who engage in a strike generally are entitled under state law to be paid all wages accrued prior to the strike. Additionally, employees who honor a picket line of another union are considered to be sympathy strikers, and, therefore, would normally not be entitled to their own accrued wages. Their wages are determined on the same basis as the primary strikers since they stand in the shoes of the primary strikers.

(2)   Unemployment Compensation Benefits.

Recently several governmental programs have become available to strikers. Strikers are generally denied unemployment compensation benefits but should an employer decide to operate during a strike, special rules may apply. play. Because of the potential impact of these benefits, the employer should carefully examine the specific laws and judicial decisions of the state in which the employer has operations. At least two states, New York and Rhode Island, specifically allow strikers to receive unemployment benefits. Under the laws of these two states, strikers must wait a specified number of weeks after the start of a strike to begin collecting benefits.

In other states, if an employee is not voluntarily working because he is participating in a labor dispute, he is not entitled to unemployment compensation. Whether an employer is operating during the strike is not important in determining whether or not employees receive unemployment compensation in these states. Please note that this issue concerning the availability of unemployment compensation benefits to striking employees must be analyzed on a state-by-state basis.

Most states generally adopt a "stoppage of work" approach when determining eligibility for unemployment compensation. These states focus on whether a given labor dispute has caused a work stoppage at the <u>employer's place of business</u> rather than on a work stoppage by the <u>individual employee</u>. Essentially, this approach involves a two-fold analysis beginning with a determination of whether a labor dispute exists followed by a determination of whether the given labor dispute has resulted in a work stoppage at the employer's place of business. If it is found that a labor dispute results in a work stoppage, any employee not employed because of the dispute may not receive unemployment benefits. Alternatively, if a work stoppage does not occur, employees not working because of the dispute may receive benefits. In either case, work must be available for the striking employees to perform in order to disqualify those employees from unemployment benefits.

Therefore, what constitutes a work stoppage and the availability of work must be determined. If an employer, through supervisory, managerial or replacement personnel, can operate the plant at normal capacity, no work stoppage results and striking employees may be entitled to benefits. At less than capacity, the results will vary. Once again, the employer should look to the relevant state guidelines in this area.

(3) Bonus Benefits for Working.

Generally employers engage in an unfair labor practice where bonus arrangements are administered to discourage union participation in a work stoppage situation. Specifically, conferring higher than normal wage payments to non-striking employees has an unlawful tendency to impact on the future exercise of the employee's right to strike. Normally, the payment of bonuses during a strike should be avoided.

However, the NLRB recently upheld one type of bonus arrangement. The employer did not violate Section 8(a)(1) of the NLRA when it paid double wages to non-strikers for days they worked during the strike. The employer's legitimate business necessity to induce non-strikers to continue production and to soothe them for harassment outweighed the coercive effect of payments on strikers. In addition, payment of extra wages was suggested by the employees, rather than by management; payments were also instituted after initiation of the strike and thus had no tendency to deter participation in the strike. Huck Manufacturing Co. v. NLRB, 693 F.2d 1176, 112 LRRM 2245 (5th Cir. 1982).

Additionally, the NLRB recently upheld another bonus arrangement whereby employees actively employed on the date of contract ratification would receive a bonus which was computed on the basis of hours worked during the strike period and was smaller for employees who participated in the strike for its duration. Crown Zellerbach Corp., 113 LRRM 1121 (1983).

(4)   Supervisory Compensation

It should be evident that the success or failure of the company to handle a strike is dependent upon the personal and coordinated efforts of the management team. However, all of the management force will be called on for long hours and great dedication during the strike. These people should be rewarded financially for the extra work that they complete during the strike. Bonuses to these people, paid during or after the strike, should be seriously considered. Remember, too, that some payroll monies may be saved during the strike, and these funds can be used to compensate these people who kept the company on its feet during the strike.

(5)   Replacement Workers

As a practical matter replacement workers should be told they will be paid at the wage rates specified in the employer's final offer to the union. These workers can be paid a specified monetary figure above or below the rates in effect under the expired contract. Fringe benefits and other terms of employment will be the same as under the expired union contract unless they were specifically changed in the employer's final offer. Employees should treat the implementation of all aspects of the final offer consistently.

b.   Benefits -- Impact of Strike on Paid Benefits.

Generally, the critical issue surrounding fringe benefit payments during a strike is whether or not the benefits
which must be paid have accrued at the time of the strike.
Typically the benefit which is deprived must have been one
which has not accrued to the employee's benefit. If the
benefit has accrued and has not been paid, the burden is on
the employer to come forward with a valid business justification for the discriminatory conduct. An analysis of the
employer's duty to pay fringe benefits will indicate that
the employer must be careful when terminating benefits of
striking employees. The most severe consequence of com-
mitting an unfair labor practice in this situation is a
possibility of converting an economic strike into an unfair
labor practice strike. Practically speaking, an employer
who is contemplating the termination of benefits should
analyze whether or not the action is worth the unfair labor
practice risk and potential legal expense. Further, it may
be better strike strategy to pay the benefits and "get the
monies spent" as early in the strike as possible rather
than giving the union another issue around which to rally
employee solidarity against the company's bargaining position. However, the proper solution in each case depends

upon a close examination of the facts, the nature of the previous contractual relationship between the parties, and the method of administration of the benefit package. The following sections further defines the specific benefit rules:

(1)   Vacation Benefits.

If under the contract entitlement to vacation time is based on net credited service, the time during a labor dispute when an involved employee is not at work need not be considered when computing vacation benefits. However, if under the contract vacation entitlement is based only on service or seniority an employer may be required to count the employee's time off when computing entitlement to vacation benefits. Finally, an employer's right to reschedule vacations or deny vacations during a strike depends upon the interpretation of the relevant agreement, past practice, and business justification for the action. Based on the relationship between the parties it may be important strike strategy to determine whether to pay the vacation benefits as early in the strike as possible or to delay payments.

(2)   Long Term Disability.

An employer is justified in terminating disability payments to employees unable to work at the start of a strike, provided the employer can show that it has acquired information which indicates that the employees, whose benefits were to be terminated, have affirmatively acted to show public support for the strike.

The NLRB recently refined the remedy for an employer violation of non-payment of LTD benefits. Now, an employee whose disability benefits are unlawfully stopped at the beginning of a strike is entitled to such benefits for a period from the beginning of the strike until either the disability that was the basis for the benefits ends or the contractual right to receive such benefits runs out, whichever comes first. The cessation of LTD benefits could be a volatile issue in the strike and could turn public support in favor of the injured employee.

3.   Holiday Pay.

Holiday pay is construed as part of wages and there-fore, strikers would normally not be entitled to such pay. However, whether laid-off employees and sympathy strikers who are covered by other bargaining agreements have the right to receive holiday pay could depend upon an interpretation of the appropriate contract provision and the past practices of the parties. For example, some agreements require that an employee work certain shifts or days (i.e., the day before and/or after the strike) in order to receive holiday pay. It has been held that under this type of labor agreements, employees are not entitled to pay if they have failed to work the required shifts because of their direct or indirect participation in a labor dispute.

(4) Sick Pay.

Similarly, an employer may not deny sick leave benefits to disabled employees at the start of an economic strike unless the employer can establish that the employees, whose benefits it seeks to discontinue, have demonstrated some "public support" for the strike. In addition, an employer cannot require employees who are sick at the time of a strike to expressly repudiate the strike in order to retain their sickness benefits. Naturally, any striker who was not sick prior to the strike will have the burden to prove his/her illness and non-participation in the strike.

c.   Implementation of Wages, Fringe Benefits and
     Work Rules.

During the course of negotiations, an employer may wish
to "suspend" talks with the union perhaps out of frustra-
tion and unilaterally implement its proposals on the work
force. As a general rule, unilateral changes in the terms
and conditions of employment instituted by an employer
during contract negotiations without consultation with the
union constitutes a failure to bargain under Section
8(a)(5) of the NLRA. The principal exception to this rule
occurs when the negotiations reach an impasse. Impasse has
been defined as "a state of facts in which the parties,
despite the best of faith, are simply deadlocked."
Determination of impasse, which depends on the mental state
of the parties, is a highly subjective inquiry. As such,
the issue is not particularly amenable to the expertise of
the NLRB as an investigative agency. Because the NLRB is
not present during the negotiations, it is difficult for
the agency to evaluate the intent of the parties. Precise
bargaining notes and lawful bargaining are essential ingredients for proof by management that an impasse exists.

If impasse has been determined, the employer is free to
implement changes in employment terms unilaterally as long

as the changes have been previously offered to the union in good faith during the recent bargaining. Naturally the employer would be required to have timely given the afore-mentioned Section 8(d) notice on Form FMCS F-7 (see Appendix C).

5. Use of Supervisory and Managerial Employees as Replacement Workers.

The effective use of supervisory and managerial employers as replacement workers is an important considera-tion when evaluating an employer's capacity to take a strike. Legally, an employer may require management and supervisory personnel to continue working during a labor dispute. Members of management have been held not to be "employees" within the meaning of the NLRA. Consequently, management does not have the rights afforded employees under the NLRA, such as honoring a picket line. Additionally, the NLRA expressly excludes supervisors from the definition of "employee." (Appendix B) As a result, an employer does not commit an unfair labor practice when discharging or disciplining managerial or supervisory per-sonnel who refuse to perform work during a strike regard-less of whether the work is supervisory or non-supervisory in nature.

As a practical consideration, the capacity and willingness of management and supervisory personnel to operate with a reduced workforce and to train any replacements under strike conditions is crucial to the ability of an employer to survive a prolonged strike. This ability to quickly and efficiently train replacement personnel and the ability to adapt to the immediate production requirements of the company are often determinative of an employer's ability to prevail in a strike.

6. **Rights of Union and Non-Union Employees to Cross the Picket Line.**

   a. **Safety Considerations.**

The general public's exposure to a strike is usually not centered on behind the scenes negotiations, but rather focused on the daily happenings along the picket line. Employees who do attempt to cross the picket line are subject to personal threats and bodily injury. To protect these employees, the employer must be aware of the general rights of union and non-union employees to cross the line. One Circuit Court of Appeals has recently reversed the NLRB and held that non-union employees who refuse to cross a picket line set up by unionized fellow employees may be treated as economic workers and permanently replaced.

Non-union employees do have the right to cross the picket line without being subject to personal threats or bodily injury from the striking employees. However, as a safety consideration, the employer should instruct non-union employees on how to safely cross the picket line. A letter should be written in advance of the strike deadline outlining procedures to be followed in reporting to work and what to do if prevented from crossing the line. The employer should advise non-striking employees as to which plant gates they should use or should not use either because they will be locked or because they are reserved for other personnel.

Specifically, picket lines should be crossed in an automobile rather than on foot whenever possible. The employee should approach and cross the picket line cautiously and at a slow rate of speed. The employee should also avoid extended conversations with pickets at the picket lines. If detained by pickets, the employee should attempt to identify the persons involved and make careful notes of the incident (see Appendix J). In addition, plant guards should be stationed at all open gates to ensure safe access to the plant. The presence of observers at the entrance gates may also facilitate employee access to the plant.

On the other hand, the employer should plan to operate during the strike on the assumption that no unionized personnel will cross the picket line. However, an employer may lawfully inquire of each employee as to their intention regarding working during the strike provided the inquiry is made to determine staffing needs. Union employees do have some rights in crossing the established picket line. For instance, a union employee may cross the picket line if that employee has made an unconditional offer to return to work and a position is available. Additionally, courts have been reluctant to extend a union's internal authority to include control over individuals who have resigned from the union. Therefore, where union members resigned and crossed a legal picket line to return to work, courts have held that the union had no authority to impose fines on these individuals. Thus, resignation from the union and subsequent return to work will afford the employee the right to cross the picket line.

However, where the union employee has neither made an unconditional offer to return to work nor resigned from union membership, the employer generally has the right not to allow striking members to enter the plant due to the possibility of sabotage, vandalism or looting. Specifically, an employer's refusal to allow striking workers to re-enter the plant and remove their tools was held not "inherently destructive" of any employee rights, where workers were given an opportunity before the strike to remove the tools, the strike was short, and the tool retention policy had no long-term effect on the strikers.

     b.   Union Options.

As mentioned above, courts have recognized that as long as an employee is a member of the union, he is subject to the union's internal rules. One internal rule frequently promulgated in union constitutions is the discipline of union members for crossing a picket line in defiance of the union. Generally, a union does not commit an unfair labor practice by threatening and imposing fines against rank-and-file union members who cross the union's picket line and work during an authorized, lawful, economic strike against an employer. On the other hand, a union may not lawfully discipline employees for crossing a picket line during a strike which is in violation of a no-strike clause or which is illegal or unprotected. Also, a union violates federal law by threatening to collect fines to enforce a signed agreement between the union and the employee to honor a strike called against an employer following the expiration of the collective bargaining agreement. Further, unions may not discipline strike-breakers by forcing an employer to take retaliatory action against them.

Threats of physical violence against strike-breakers is another union option in maintaining striker solidarity. However, NLRB decisions hold that threats of physical violence by a union against a member for refusal to cooperate in strike activities violates Section 8(b)(1)(A) of the NLRA.

While it is clear that an employer may utilize supervisors to perform struck work, a union may discipline its supervisor-members for performing certain types of work during a strike. Specifically, union discipline of its supervisor-members for crossing picket lines and performing rank-and-file struck work (work normally performed by striking, non-supervisory employees) during a lawful economic strike is not a violation. Further, a union is not in violation of federal law by fining supervisor-members who spend more than a minimal amount of time performing struck bargaining unit work while working inside a picket line.

Conversely, a union does commit an unfair labor practice by disciplining supervisor-members for working behind a picket line where the supervisors perform principally supervisory functions, although they may also perform a minimal amount of rank-and-file work. Essentially, the current state of the law only allows unions to discipline supervisor-members who cross the picket line to perform struck bargaining unit work and not supervisory functions.

7. Protection of Company Property.

A principal concern of an employer during a strike is the possibility of injury to its employees and damage to company property. This problem increases when strike conditions give rise to looting, arson, vandalism and/or other forms of violence. Therefore, the employer should take measures to protect employees, company property and operations based on the assumption that such violence may occur. Whenever a union guarantee as to the security of the premises and undisturbed access to non-striking personnel cannot be obtained, or when doubt exists as to the safety of employees or property, maximum security measures should be taken. The following areas should be considered:

a. Security Services.

Many employers utilize professional security support services. These companies specialize in the protection of employees and company assets during an emergency. Services are provided by trained professionals whose experience in these situations afford an employer a maximum degree of protection without intimidation to the employer's striking workers who may eventually return to work.

Depending upon the particular employer requirements, the security service will provide a comprehensive on-site survey and provide a staff of physical security and support service personnel to work with the employer in devising an effective security plan. Additionally, these services will provide patrol service, communications, investigative support, photographic surveillance, executive protection, meals and rest facilities.

b. Controlled Entrances.

Guaranteeing free and safe access to the buildings for supervisors and non-striking employees can become a difficult problem for management. Depending on the physical arrangement of the work area and the nature of the strike, the employer may choose to keep only a few entrances open. For instance, in a large building this may entail denying public access to all floors except the main floor, the closing off of elevators not likely to be used and shutting down of boilers in the heating plant. Entrances may be limited to one or two doors while any pick up or delivery service may also be restricted to certain entrances. All unused doors and gates should be closed and locked. Locks at the edge-of-premises doors and gates may need to be changed to prevent their unauthorized opening. Designated employees should see that back doors are locked, lights are turned off and windows closed at the end of each day. A log must be kept of all vehicles and persons entering onto company property during the strike (See Appendix I).

8. Injunctive Relief.

Legal action in a strike situation is frequently time-consuming and expensive and may be damaging to the long-term employment relationship. The idea of judicial intervention is one, like so many other strike-related concerns, that must be considered in advance.

By judicial intervention, what is most often meant is injunctive relief. An injunction is an order of a court (state or federal) to the party to whom it is addressed, demanding that party refrain from proceeding in the actions or course of conduct specified therein. An injunction will normally be granted to prevent irreparable harm to the parties or to protect the health, welfare, and safety of the public. Injunctions are a last resort, stopgap measure and are not easily obtained.

The availability of injunctive relief is an important employer option. Generally, an employer may bring an action to enjoin violent, intimidating, or coercive conduct by striking employees. Depending on the facts and circumstances of the case, an injunction may be issued against a union or employees who have violated a no-strike provision in the collective bargaining agreement. An employer's choice of judicial forums in which to seek an injunction are generally dictated by the conduct the company wants to enjoin, i.e., illegal strikes or picket line violence. Before proceeding with a request for injunctive relief, an employer should consult with legal counsel concerning the relative advantages and disadvantages, substantative and procedural, in pursuing injunctive relief in the state or federal courts. The employer will also have several legal options through the NLRB.

a. Illegal Strikes

In its landmark Boys' Market decision, the United States Supreme Court held that the Norris-LaGuardia Act did not prohibit federal district courts from enjoining a strike which violated a no-strike clause in a collective bargaining agreement. In order to enjoin an illegal strike, the collective bargaining agreement must provide for mandatory arbitration of the dispute underlying the job action. The three jurisdictional prerequisites to enjoining an illegal strike before a federal district court are:

1. The strike must be in violation of a no-strike clause in the current collective bargaining agreement; and

2. The strike must be over an arbitrable grievance; and

3. Both parties must be contractually bound to arbitrate the grievance which caused the strike.

Since the Boys' Market decision, federal courts have been given the authority to enjoin a strike in breach of a no-strike provision. However, an express no-strike clause in the current collective bargaining agreement is not required before injunctive relief will be granted. Courts have ruled that a contract providing for final and binding arbitration of labor disputes creates an implied obligation not to strike over such disputes.

b. Picket Line Violence

Violent, intimidating, or coercive conduct by employees engaged in a strike is generally prohibited under most state laws. Although the scope and nature of illegal picket line activity differs from state to state, statutory provisions generally forbid mass picketing, blocking of ingress or egress, violence or threats of violence against customers and non-striking employees, and/or interfering with common carriers.

Whether a court will grant injunctive relief depends on the specific facts of each case. Before seeking a court order to bring an end to striking employee misconduct, an employer must present concrete evidence to support his argument for an injunction. Usually the employer is required to show that the misconduct has occurred and is illegal, that the misconduct will continue if the court does not intervene, and that the employer will suffer irreparable harm if an injunction is not issued. Although this places a difficult burden upon the employer, careful planning and documentation can help ease this burden.

As noted, the issuance of an injunction depends on the strength of the evidence presented. An employer should adopt procedures for gathering and preserving all evidence of employee misconduct. (See Appendices I and J). However, in formulating and carrying out these procedures, an employer must be careful not to violate Section 8(a)(1) of the NLRA. This section prohibits an employer from interfering with, restraining or coercing employees engaged in a strike.

To avoid allegations of unfair labor practices by striking employees, an employer should develop a plan for overseeing, photographing if appropriate and logging picket line activity. Without proper documentation of striking employee violence or misconduct, the employer will find it nearly impossible to get an injunction in either the state or federal court. On the other hand, unless the employer can show "just cause", monitoring of strikers engaged in picketing may constitute illegal interference and coercion of employees and their right to strike. An overall plan to monitor picket line activity is useful not only in substantiating a request for injunctive relief but also in unfair labor practice proceedings with the NLRB.

An employer is permitted to engage in picket line surveillance for the purpose of gathering evidence in order to obtain an injunction to halt illegal strike activity. However, in the absence of picket line violence or unlawful strike activity, an employer must have sufficient evidence to support surveillance of the picket line. Before proceeding with surveillance procedures, the employer must have reason to expect picket line violence or illegal strike activity, and be able to document his expectations and anxieties. Evidence of prior illegal strikes or picket line violence in prior strikes may be sufficient to persuade a court to issue an injunction.

An injunction when issued should contain specific restrictions as to the time, place, and manner in which striking employees may picket. Specific injunction language is more desirable for two reasons. First, the use of specific restrictions will not have the overwhelming negative impact on the strikers as general prohibitions may have. Secondly, violations of specific prohibitions are easier to prove which, in turn, should reduce the potential for disruptive conduct on the picket lines in violation of an injunctive order.

Another important item which must be covered by the management team in devising its strategy for enjoining picket line violence is communication with law enforcement officials. An injunction will be of no use unless the police enforce its provisions. The police may add insights into the potential effectiveness of this legal remedy. Leaving these officials out in the cold on important decisions concerning the conduct of striking employees generally will result in either an inability or a refusal to enforce the provisions of the injunction.

   c.   Choice of Forum.

Federal law does not divest state courts of their jurisdiction over a suit for the violation of a contract between an employer and a labor organization. State courts have concurrent jurisdiction in actions for violations of collective bargaining agreements. This concurrent jurisdiction extends to the issuance of injunctive orders. Suits for contract violations and proceedings to enjoin picket line violence and misconduct may be brought in either the state or federal court. The appropriate choice of the two forums depends on the circumstances of the case and an analysis of the local judiciary.

Although the employer may petition a state court for injunctive relief against violence during a strike, the NLRB may, in the proper circumstances, request the injunction in a federal court. Furthermore, the Board and the federal courts are concerned with illegal secondary boycotts, and unlawful picket line activities. Federal action, absent one of these two situations, is not a viable option. The employer may always request the NLRB to petition for an injunction, but the NLRB alone will determine whether or not to seek an injunction. The employer may not seek an injunction in federal court except if the strike is in violation of a no-strike clause. He may, however, seek a state court injunction to enjoin any violent activity. State court injunctions are often liberally granted if the strike threatens violence or the public safety or welfare of the community. However, the standards vary from state to state and often from judge to judge. This is why there is a great deal of discretion in deciding whether to seek an injunction and the forum in which it will be sought.

The federal district court in which the facility is located is the federal court authorized to grant an injunction in a strike matter. Federal court judges are appointed for life. Because federal judges do not stand for reelection, they do not have the same concerns about how their constituents will react to an injunction order. In theory, federal judges are less concerned politically -- i.e., with seeking votes -- than are state court judges. Some federal judges are more sympathetic to the feelings and reactions of other influential government officials than are state court judges. Frequently, state court judges will refuse to issue strike injunctions or to rule on the motion because they fear alienating a strong pro-union constituency. In such cases, the matter should be assigned to a state court judge from another community. On other occasions, a state court judge may try to act as a mediator, sometimes with good results. All of these factors must be considered before involvement in any court action.

Procedurally, union officials must be served with legal process giving notice of the injunction request. The names and addresses of all union members should also be prepared well in advance. Federal law requires that notice be given, in a manner as the court directs, to all persons against whom relief is sought and to chief public officials of the county and city in which the unlawful acts have been threatened or committed. Specifically, the notice requirement refers to a hearing on a preliminary or permanent injunction. Temporary restraining orders will usually be issued without notice.

d. Use of NLRB Procedures.

In order to obtain an injunction in federal court through the NLRB, documentation of picket line violence is essential. Proof of an incident means securing pictures, video tapes, films, and/or affidavits of the individuals involved. All of these devices for substantiating the occurrence of an event must be prepared and ready for use at the outset of any incident. Once documentation is gathered, an unfair labor practice charge may be filed at the appropriate NLRB office. This preliminary step is the prerequisite for the NLRB to seek injunctive relief. The charge should be filed by a knowledgeable company official, and the documentation underlying the charge brought to the NLRB's immediate attention. An NLRB charge seeking injunctive relief receives priority investigation by the NLRB and routinely will be investigated within 48 hours of its filing. NLRB investigators will come to the plant and interview people, inspect the layout, observe any damage, and check with the union as to its position on the allegations. Because of the time limitations involved, it is best for the company to help the investigation along and provide all available information when a charge if filed. Affidavits, witnesses, and physical evidence should be made readily accessible to the NLRB. If the investigation concludes in a finding of reasonable cause to believe the union is violating the NLRA, then the Board will seek to enjoin the strike activities in the appropriate U.S. district court if the violence continues after a charge is filed. The NLRB will prepare and file all relevant documents. The NLRB attorneys will represent the employer's interest in court once the NLRB Regional Office has decided to seek an injunction. It is a strategic advantage to have the federal government on your side and it is also a significant cost savings to the employer. The NLRA, at

Section 10(i), provides that these requests for injunctive relief be handled expeditiously and, if possible, within ten (10) days of docketing. This time schedule may be shortened when a temporary restraining order is sought. A temporary restraining order may be granted ex parte, without notice to the other side. Once it is granted, as with an injunction, the union must have actual notice of the terms of the order for it to be used as the basis in a subsequent contempt proceeding. To give actual notice, service of process is required. To enforce the order through contempt proceedings, the employer must notify the NLRB of any violations.

Relief available from injunctions and temporary restraining orders is limited to enjoining, or ceasing, certain conduct by the union or individuals acting in concert. However, these remedies make no provision for damages. Therefore, individuals who have been injured during a strike will have to bring actions in state court to recover their damages for personal injury or damages to their property.

Criminal complaints should be filed and arrests sought when picket line violence or sabotage surfaces. Failure of the local police to take action is the basis for urging the NLRB to step in and seek an injunction in federal court.

9. Continuing Duty To Bargain.

Even though a strike has commenced, both parties have a continuing duty to bargain. A number of bargaining strategies may be utilized during the strike depending on the course of negotiations. These strategies should significantly influence the tone and direction of each session and aim to provide management with the upper hand during negotiations. Good negotiations strategy and thorough preparation are more important than ever if the company engages in bargaining during a walkout. However, the actual negotiating posture of management once a strike has commenced depends upon the long term result which management hopes to achieve by taking the strike.

a. Long Term Game Plan.

(1) Decertification.

The likelihood of decertification after the strike is resolved depends in large part on the use of replacement workers. The more replacement workers hired, the less chance that returning economic strikers may regain their old positions. Further, these replacement workers may then vote to decertify the union in the next election. The timing of the decertification petition (employee filed--RD petition or employer filed--RM petition) with the NLRB depends upon the expiration date of the contract and the status of bargaining. Employees may also consider filing a deauthorization petition (UD petition) with the NLRB. This petition cuts off the union dues checkoff (union security) requirement.

The decision to replace strikers may seriously affect management's negotiating posture during the strike. Management could take a much harder line in responding to union demands. Management would also be less likely to compromise on issues involving job security since it has made the decision to operate indefinitely through the use of replacement workers. However, a long term goal of decertification should only be made after careful consideration of the effect of the decision on picket line behavior. Fearing loss of membership, the union may promote the escalation of harrassment and violence on the picket line. Management must be prepared to provide safe passage across the picket line for these replacement workers. Management should also be prepared to respond to "union busting" allegations because they hired "scabs" as replacement workers.

(2) Strike.

Another long term strike goal involves the continued operation of the company utilizing management and supervisory personnel during the strike. The proven willingness and ability of management to operate during a strike should enhance the credibility of its implicit threat of an unsuccessful union strike in future situations. The result may be a greater reluctance on the part of workers to resort to strike action and more interest in compromise and accommodation at the bargaining table. Management can show, by graphic illustration to the employees, the cost of the strike. Appendix P shows the cost of each day of the strike to the employees. When faced with an economic strike this highlights the absurdity of a prolonged strike for higher wages.

Both parties may be more willing to compromise knowing that the returning strikers will eventually be returned to their former positions. Consequently, this option lessens the likelihood of post-strike decertification.

Essentially, the negotiating posture in this situation is dictated by the decision to take the strike rather than break the union.

(3) Cost to the Company.

The cost of a strike is a fundamental consideration prior to a determination of whether to take a strike or avoid a strike by granting the union's demands. These costs include both monetary and non-monetary considerations. Initially, the company must assess its position from an economic standpoint. Management must assess its present inventory position, its production capabilities and the market position of the company. If management determines that taking a strike will not substantially impair the ability to continue operating profitably, the decision to operate will be a legitimate option.

However, the growth of domestic and foreign non-union competition in some industries has raised the cost of strikes to management in terms of both loss of sales in the short run and market share in the long run. Additionally, increasing union recourse to such tactics as coalition bargaining and selective strikes, together with the growing ability of employees to withstand long strikes, raises the cost at the bargaining table. The company must weigh these monetary factors to arrive at a decision which is in the best interest of the company.

Additionally, less tangible considerations must be addressed prior to a decision. For example, the employer must consider the public relations aspect. Will the decision to operate be seen as an unwarranted union-busting scheme or will the public react favorably to the company's stand? Also, the concerns of both non-union employees and non-striking union employees must be considered. Will the company lose the respect of and willingness to work of these workers should management cave in to union demands? These concerns, albeit nonmonetary, are just as important as profit considerations in determining the cost to the company of taking and/or continuing a strike.

IV. COMMUNICATIONS AND PUBLIC RELATIONS ASPECTS OF THE STRIKE

Public relations is probably the most overlooked area in a strike, yet in the final analysis this crucial aspect of a strike will probably determine how soon the strike will end. The employer must establish a public relations function both internally and externally. This function

-111-

includes communications with employees, the union and the general public. Internal lines of communication are indispensible to sound employee morale and to the decision-making process. Conversely, external communications project the employer's image to the community and the general public.

Therefore, a good communications plan, within the company and outside, is a continual process and not a makeshift operation to be suddenly implemented in an emergency. A plan initiated after a crisis begins will appear self-serving and suspect.

A. Communicating with Your Workforce.

   1. Before the Impasse.

Management should strive to communicate with employees at all times and not only in periods of crisis. When employees know the rationale behind the management decisions affecting them, they are more likely to cooperate fully in carrying out these decisions. Therefore, it is imperative that employees be kept abreast of the status of any negotiations between the management and the employee organization. During negotiations, the rank and file

-112-

employees are only informed as to what the union bargaining team wants them to hear.

Generally when a strike becomes a near certainty, it may be worthwhile for the employer to send a personal letter to every employee, addressed to the home, informing the employee as to the present status of negotiations, the issues causing the impasse, management's position on these issues and the reasons for the position. Many times these communications are addressed to the employee and spouse in an attempt to make the strike decision a family decision. The substance of this information could also be transmitted through additional meetings called by supervisors, special bulletins, and posted memoranda.

A note of caution is in order. The law prohibits employer communications that are intended to undermine or bypass the union as the employees' exclusive collective bargaining representative. This prohibition extends to threats or promises that are intended to diminish support for the union among employees. For example, employers have acted unlawfully when they offer directly to employees, during negotiations, a contract of greater economic value than any previously offered to the union. It is also unlawful to misrepresent the union's bargaining position to the employees by implying that the union's contract proposals were in some respect adverse to their interest, and then suggest that the employees decide among themselves whether they should sign the contract. However, the employer has been held not to have "undermined the union" when management has accurately informed employees of the status of negotiations and stated the employer's position; asked the employees to vote to accept the employer's final offer when it was presented for ratification; clarified confusion as to certain contract proposals; answered employee questions involving interpretations of the proposed contract; and/or informed employees of the employer's concern over the possibility of a work stoppage.

2.   Under the Strike.

Similarly, any communications seen as an attempt by an employer to threaten or induce employees to leave the union or to abandon their bargaining agent during the course of a strike will be viewed as an unfair labor practice. Once again, the employer must carefully word any communication to the employees during a strike so as not to "undermine" the union.   For example, the employer should not even suggest to striking employees that they resign or withdraw from the union or repudiate the union as their bargaining representative. The employer should not assist employees who want to resign or withdraw from the union, or to call an internal union vote to end the strike. Lastly, an employer should not offer or grant any benefit such as higher wages, super-seniority, shorter hours or free meals, to induce striking employees to return to work. Conversely, an employer may communicate more freely and liberally to the remaining personnel acting as the "workforce" during the course of a strike.

a.   Status of Ongoing Negotiations.

All operating personnel should be kept informed of developments throughout the negotiations. Morale may suffer if the strikers learn, through their negotiators, of developments before the operating personnel learn of them from management. Information should be passed to the workforce through meetings or short bulletins. This information should cover the union's demands, the employer's counterproposals, and progress in both negotiations and production. It is especially important that supervisors remain in the employer's confidence. Supervisors may often be the only link with the strikers. Therefore, supervisors may be in the best position to provide management with information concerning attitudes, ideas and rumors which in turn may be valuable in reaching an early settlement.

b. Impact of the Strike Upon the Employees of the Company and Their Families.

An important consideration too often overlooked in a strike setting is the strike's devastating impact on the employees and their families. The uncertainty of the negotiations and pervading atmosphere of threats, hostility and violence place a terrible strain on many personal relationships. Therefore, the employer should take steps to keep families of working employees informed as to the strike issues. For example, an employer could establish an internal telephone message system for employees and their families to call and receive a recorded information update. Frequently this also serves as a rumor control mechanism. Top management personnel should maintain visibility and accessibility to working employees and their families. These considerate actions may be beneficial, from a morale standpoint, to the families, especially when the employees are spending long hours in the plant.

B. Informing Your Suppliers, Deliverers, Customers.

1. Pick-up, Deliveries and Sales.

Though reaching a settlement through negotiations is of paramount interest to an employer, the regular operations of the company may not be neglected. Therefore, to facilitate the continuity of operations, the employer should compile a list of current customers and suppliers providing essential materials and services to the employer. Alternate sources for these products and services should also be identified and contacted since unionized employees of suppliers may refuse to cross the picket line. Management should then take immediate steps to notify these suppliers and deliverers of the impending strike or a strike in progress. Additionally, management should do as much as possible to reassure its customers that everything possible will be done to provide timely and complete service to them. The customers should also be informed of the employer's bargaining position with the employee organization and the employer's desire to maintain service.

2. <u>Relationship with the Local Community</u>.

The local community is perhaps the most important re-
cipient of the employer's communications efforts. There is
a strong tendency to cater to the large news sources
because of their vast coverage, but the key to any strike
is the local media and their influence on the local public.
The employer should place its communications emphasis on
the local media in order to enhance its position in the
community once the strike is resolved. Therefore, prior to
the strike, the communications coordinator should locate
the "opinion leaders" in the community and see to it that
they are informed as to the problems facing the employer.
During the strike, these same people should be kept abreast
of all developments in the strike and should be given data
to support the employer's position.

a. <u>Press Releases</u>.

One effective method for communicating with the public
is through the use of timely press releases. The
employer's spokesperson should use the press release as a
forum for communicating the facts. It is advised that all
releases should be cleared through the company negotiators

and legal counsel. It should never be used to instigate a direct attack on the employees or employee organization. Remember that after the strike is over, anything management says will have a permanent affect on its continuing relationship with the union.

b. <u>Public Appearances.</u>

Another technique for galvanizing local community support is through public appearances. The employer should be willing to communicate the message that it is willing to negotiate with the union to try and reach an agreement at any time. Therefore, an employer spokesperson, usually the communications coordinator, should be available to appear on television to accurately portray the employer's position in the labor dispute. Additionally, this spokesperson should be available to represent the employer at local organization meetings such as the city council, Lions, Kiwanis, and Rotary Clubs. Once again, to maintain the company's credibility, it would be wise not to attack any personalities, but rather attack the validity of the union's position during the course of these public appearances. Management should explain why it has taken the position that it has in bargaining.

c.   <u>Ads in the Paper</u>.

Another effective method for establishing a credible
relationship with the local community and all interested
parties is through the use of advertisements in the local
newspapers. Unlike a single television or radio spot, the
use of newspaper advertisements enables an employer to present the reader with a great deal of information at once.
The format of the ad itself should be in summary form while
highlighting the major issues involved in the dispute. The
use of bold print in strategic areas will help to attract
the reader to vital facts. A typical advertisement might
include a short synopsis of the current negotiations status. The employer may also wish to include a short history
of the company, an overview of the company's business
industry and why changes are needed to compete in this
industry. Also, it is a good idea to outline the major
issues involved in the dispute highlighting the company's
position while addressing any rumors which have reached the
company's attention. In general, the employer should
always stress the reasonableness of its position on major
points of disagreement. Done correctly, an advertisement
can be an effective tool in building credibility and a

favorable reputation with the local community. Appendix D is a recent strike advertisement which highlights the relevant strike issues and facts.

C. Relationship with the Press/Media.

An employer must effectively communicate its position regarding strategic issues in the labor dispute to a wide variety of audiences. The easiest way to reach all of these groups is through the media. There are several techniques which are helpful in implementing an effective overall media strategy.

Good press relations can be fostered by establishing a communication center for news reports and press briefings. If the media comes to the company premises and finds nothing but the confusion which usually accompanies a strike, the press is not likely to give the company favorable press coverage. The communications center could consist of at least a press room with outgoing phone lines, the latest press releases and background material. The purpose of the center is to provide a location where the media can get credible material concerning the number of employees on strike, the status of negotiations, continued operations and other background information. In addition,

-121-

the center can be used as a place for the employer to discover what types of information the press is interested in and what information is being disseminated by the union.

Members of the local press may have little experience in covering labor negotiations or labor disputes. Inexperience and lack of familiarity with labor terms can lead to inaccurate and misleading coverage. To avoid this problem, the employer should initiate background briefings for members of the local press. The spokesperson should be ready to explain any confusing terms in simple and concise language. Similarly, the spokesperson should also explain the nature of any confusing issues posing obstacles to settlement. These initial briefings can produce a dramatic improvement in the quality of the news coverage of the strike and negotiations. Therefore, education of the press should begin immediately after the strike and should continue as necessitated by the situation, until a settlement is reached. The employer should always be as objective as possible regarding the union's position on any particular issue. Gaining and sustaining the trust and confidence of members of the press is as important to the employer's position as intelligent and comprehensive news coverage. Finally, the spokesperson should impress upon the media the fact that the employer is making every effort to settle the strike as quickly and equitably as possible. An employer's effort to settle the labor dispute while maintaining its reputation with the community can only be achieved by working closely and harmoniously with members of the media.

D. Proper Utilization of State or Federal Mediator

During the course of any strike or labor dispute, particularly one of long duration, it is not unusual for the parties involved to mutually desire to settle the contract dispute. However, as the strike continues, various problems arise which add to the complexity of settling the dispute. Economic drives, emotions, human relations problems, breakdown of communications, public relations postures, intra-company and union politics all become entangled in the dispute. Too often the fundamental issues which gave rise to the initial disagreement are obscured by these peripheral matters. Consequently, a labor mediator, whether federal or state, may best serve as a catalyst to revive negotiations and hasten the end of the strike.

The parties desire to reach agreement must be a joint desire by each side to achieve an equitable accommodation of the conflicting points of view. Each party must be

-123-

willing to be convinced of and be ready to yield to a more reasonable view advanced by the other. Absent such a desire, a mediator cannot be properly utilized.

A well trained, thoroughly prepared mediator can be an invaluable tool in reaching a satisfactory settlement. The mediator must first have an understanding and appreciation of the problems confronting the parties. This involves a complete knowledge of the field of labor and industrial relations, awareness of trends and patterns, an appreciation of any human relations problems and a working concept of the economics of the industry and company involved. The mediator will strive to ascertain the facts of the dispute and understand the position and problems of both parties. A competent mediator will then use any number of tactics to precipitate a settlement. However, unless the mediator is kept informed of the status of bargaining, he will be ineffective for a considerable period of bargaining.

For example, the mediator may generate doubt in the minds of both parties as to the validity of their respective positions. This does not entail coercive pressure on either side to retreat from their positions. Rather, it involves perceiving the employer's position on the issues, and that of the union, as symptoms of problems which the parties seek to resolve. The mediator's objective will be to persuade both parties to look at alternative ways of handling the remaining issues.

The mediator may also suggest alternative solutions, drawn from his own experience. It may well be that a major issue separating the employer and union, no matter how new and immediate it is for them, has been previously resolved by the mediator. The mediator has a vast resource of alternate solutions used successfully in the past, which may provide the springboard for a settlement.

Also, a mediator may make an informal test of possible alternatives. Each side may be unwilling to advance an alternative settlement of its own, fearing that such a pro- position may be taken as a change in position. The mediator, aided by the caucus system, can be invaluable in this regard. The mediator can shuttle between the caucus rooms presenting the other side's proposition as if it were his own suggestion. The mediator can then closely monitor the parties' reactions. Any positive response by a party could supply the wedge that breaks the logjam blocking the negotiations. The impact of an experienced "neutral" can- not be underestimated.

E.   Evaluating the Roles of the Local Police.

It is important to reach an understanding with the local police before the strike begins as to what their role will be in controlling the picket line. The police will be reluctant to get actively involved in the strike itself, but they will protect property and safety. It is important to recognize what the police can do for the employer and to express to the police force before the strike that the company expects these functions to be performed. The earlier the police department is alerted to the anticipated problems, the better prepared the police force will be in order to provide an adequate number of police officers to control the situation. The police provide the strongest force in controlling picketing situations. The police can help people enter the plant with only minimal disturbance. Yet, people cannot approach a picket line and expect an officer to let them through as if they are parting the Red Sea. The police will help to let people enter and to eliminate the propensity for violence, but it will take time. Management's ongoing contacts with the police department will probably increase as the strike progresses. Do not push the officers to do things that they do not want to do.

Make requests, explain the company's goals and objectives, and let the police handle the rest. It is sometimes advisable for both the union and management to sit down with police to iron out guidelines for protecting both sides' legitimate rights and expectations and explain how the laws will be applied. It is best to hold such a conference as soon as possible before any confrontations occur. (See Appendix G).

V. POST-STRIKE CONSIDERATIONS

A. Smooth Transition in the Aftermath.

The period immediately following the settlement of a strike may be as trying for management as the strike period itself. Numerous concerns arise at this time relating to settlement terms, threats and reprisals. The necessity of returning to normal operations as quickly and as smoothly as possible cannot be overstated. Careful, thorough planning and execution of the policies that guided the employer through the strike period will be invaluable in the post-strike period.

Post-strike attitudes of both management and the union are important in achieving a harmonious relationship.

Restoring communication channels and resolving any personality conflicts which may have contributed to earlier bad feelings may be the first steps toward a post-strike adjustment. Additionally, arrangements to comply with the terms of the agreement should be initiated as soon as possible.

Reprisals against non-striking employees and returning strikers is another concern in the transition. The union may propose a "no reprisal" clause which provides that management will not discriminate against any person who went on strike or supported the strike. If management agrees to this provision, it may have relinquished its right to take action against sabotage and violence by strikers, its right to take action against managers that supported or aided the strike, and possibly its right to deduct pay from salaries for the strike period. If management relinquishes its right to punish striking employees, the union should also be restrained from disciplining non-striking employees. Management can protect these employees by demanding an agreement banning post-strike reprisals. Accordingly, management should at the very least demand agreement on the following types of clauses:

The Union agrees that neither it nor its members
will take any action, directly or indirectly,
against any employee or person for non-participation
in the strike and strike-related activities, and
will actively seek to discourage any actions
against such people.

This no-reprisal clause shall, in no way, preclude
the withholding of direct and indirect compensation
for non-performance of service during the strike.
Nor shall this clause apply to management employees
or to any legal action against employees who committed acts of sabotage, violence or violations of
the law.

Management should take the initiative in addressing and
resolving the immediate concerns of management, the union,
and all employees following the strike. The success of the
transition between strike period confrontation and post-
strike harmony will depend in large measure on the willingness of the employer to promote an immediate peaceful
working environment.

B. Picket Line or Strike Misconduct.

Management or non-striking employes may file an unfair
labor practice charge under Section 8(b)(1)(A) of the NLRA
for any picket line misconduct. However, the employer may
wish to evaluate the success or wisdom of fully processing
a particular charge. A distinction is commonly made by the
NLRB between labor dispute (strike) violence and normal

work environment violence, with a more lenient attitude being manifested toward any strike violence. Thus, the issue becomes one of differentiating between those acts which do warrant discipline and those which do not. In order to make such a determination, arbitrators frequently utilize a set of criteria first articulated in the General Electric Co. [4] case:

1. How serious was the offense in terms of injury to persons or damage to property?

2. Was the act provoked or unprovoked?

3. Was the act a premeditated one of aggression, or was it a spur of the moment reaction to an unanticipated situation?

4. Was the conduct destructive of good employee-employer relations?

5. Was the conduct destructive of good community relations?

6. Did the conduct increase community fears and did terror result?

7. What will be the effect of the administration of the discipline?

8. Will it restore good relations?

9. Will it create a respect for law and order?

---

[4] 38 LA 1182, 1185-86 (1961)

10. Is the discipline being administered in a spirit of vindictiveness or for the purpose of establishing a "showcase"?

The answer to these questions may well provide the employer with the basis for choosing to process or not process a particular strike misconduct charge with the NLRB.

A civil trespass action is another action available to an employer when strike activities involve abusive language, harassment, or violence. When it is possible to show that an individual employee engaged in picket line misconduct, that employee may be terminated. However, recourse against the union is limited to instances wherein the employer can prove not only that the employee engaged in misconduct, but also that the union condoned the activity. The element of union condonation underscores the importance of the "Incident Report" (Appendix J).

Termination is also a possible response to wildcat or unprotected strike actions. Permanent replacement is a possibility with economic strikers, subject to preferential rehiring. When an unfair labor practice striker is replaced, his replacement is temporary, and the returning employee has a right to reinstatement within five days of an unconditional offer to return to work. Therefore, it is unwise to offer permanent employment when an unfair labor practice charge is pending. Job stability is usually an advantage in gaining replacement workers, but the liability of continuing to pay them after a settlement is reached can be significant. The possibility of severance pay or unemployment compensation benefits for these employees after the strike is over can also be an expensive consideration. The safest approach as mentioned earlier, is to merely "replace" the strikers without designating whether the replacements are temporary or permanent.

For strikes in violation of a contract and strikes which are attended by some form of violent activity, management is not limited to discharging strikers. Suspensions or letters of reprimand may also serve as a lesser form of employee discipline. The purpose of a letter is to put the strikers on notice that repeated or continued actions may lead to employer action. (Appendix E). The purpose is to tell the employees that they have a job to do and that they may be subject to replacement or discharge if the strike is in violation of a contract. Generally, if picket line misconduct is at issue, management should take a firm approach if it appears the striker has engaged in anything more than mere verbal exchanges. However, each situation must be evaluated separately. For example, management may want to consider whether the employee is a union officer, the identity of the aggrieved person and the long term ramifications of the incident.

In practice, the eventual settlement agreement will encompass or resolve most of these discipline items. Its main purpose, therefore, is strategic rather than substantive.

C. Timing of the Return to Work.

A very critical, yet often overlooked, concern of management following a strike is the timing of the return of striking employees to work. Legally, employees have five work days to report to work. Management may take the offensive and make an unconditional offer of reinstatement during the strike. The substantive nature of the offer of reinstatement must be unconditional. The employer cannot force the employees to disclose information about the union or their strike activities. Since supervisors have the closest contact with the work force, the following instructions to supervisors are suggested to smooth the transition:

1.   Greet each returning employee in such a way as to indicate that you are happy he is back at work.

2.   Avoid discussions regarding events which occurred during the strike such as violence, court cases, unfair labor practice charges and actions of individual employees or union officers.

3.   Do not in any way criticize union officers, members or strikers.

4.   It is likely that many employees were unsympathetic toward the strike. Some may have been subject to threats and coercion, which they find difficult to forget. In such cases, you as a supervisor have a real opportunity to provide guidance and leadership while improving employee relationships.

5.   Avoid becoming too friendly with either the returning striker or the non-striker. Returning strikers will undoubtedly be overly sensitive to any action that could be construed as showing partiality toward employees who stayed at work. Also be sure to consider that the employee who did not strike is in a difficult situation vis-a-vis the striker. Frequently the non-strikers have been harassed while crossing the picket line and often referred to as "scabs."

6.   Do everything possible to make sure that all employees are assigned to jobs and kept busy without giving the appearance of pushing them. This must be done quickly. Also, avoid having employees gather in groups.

7.   Be alert for unusual happenings. Make frequent trips through the department to see that everything is running properly.

8.   Make an extra effort to provide advice and assistance to employees on their jobs as required.

9.   As a strategic consideration, have the returning strikers begin work at the beginning of their shift rather than during the middle of the shift.

The employer must try to alleviate any residual bitter feelings resulting from the strike. What transpires when the striking employees return to work will serve as a barometer to the success of the transition.

D. Status of Employee Benefits.

Generally an employer, once the contract has expired, may make changes in those benefits that are not vested or specifically continued by the expired contract. Whether a returning employee is entitled to receive benefits, including sick leave and disability payments, depends on whether the benefits are judged to be deferred compensation or a form of wages. Any deferred compensation will generally be restored to a worker upon his return to work. Wage equivalent benefits may be withheld. The particular language of the collective bargaining agreement will usually determine how the benefits are to be classified.

Specifically, it has been held that an employer, by failing to grant unfair labor practice strikers who had unconditionally offered to return to work, unlawfully withheld vacation pay for which the employees would have been eligible had the employer not unlawfully failed to reinstate them. Also, it has been held that an employer violated Section 8(a)(3) of the NLRA when it treated returning strikers as "new employees" for health insurance purposes, with the result that coverage was not reinstated for 90 days. Generally, courts will find employer's actions unlawful if the disparate treatment of benefits between non-strikers and strikers has a discouraging effect on both present and future concerted activities. If the employer cannot establish a legitimate business purpose for the disparate treatment, the company's action may constitute an unfair labor practice.

E. Who Returns to Work?

1. Reinstatement Rights.

A particularly important post-strike consideration involves the decision of which striking employees have a legal right to return to an immediate position within the organization. The law recognizes two basic types of strikers for the purpose of determining reinstatement rights.

Economic strikers who have not obtained substantially equivalent employment elsewhere have a right to reinstatement upon their unconditional offer to return to work. (See Appendix O for a sample offer of reinstatement.) Additionally, in the event that no job is available at the time of reinstatement, an economic striker is entitled to an offer of reinstatement whenever a vacancy occurs that he is qualified to fill, unless (1) the employer can show legitimate and substantial business reasons to justify a failure to offer reinstatement or (2) the striker does acquire substantially equivalent employment elsewhere.

Once an unconditional offer to return to work has been made by an economic striker, the following process should be implemented to assign work to the employee. Employees must be offered remaining jobs in the order in which they offer to return. If several employees return at the same time and date, their seniority will determine the order of offering jobs within that group. Further, the employee should be given job offers in the following order. First, the employee should be offered his or her former specific job if there is an opening. If the former job is not available, the employee should next be offered a substantially equivalent job for which the employee is qualified if there is an opening. In determining "substantially equivalent" jobs, the following factors should be considered: wage rate, progression opportunity, similar nature of work, working conditions, same department and same shift.

An employee who has applied for reinstatement, but for whom there is no acceptable job available, becomes a "replaced" striker. The employee is not a laid-off employee, and except for the procedure for recall, the employee has no other rights which a laid-off employee has under the expired labor contract.

However, no new employee can be hired to replace a returning striker who has vacated a job without first offering the job to striking employees who have unconditionally applied for reinstatement and have been denied reinstatement, provided their former job was substantially equivalent to the opening.

Unfair labor practice strikers have an absolute right to reinstatement if the strike was for a lawful purpose and was lawfully conducted; and the employer is required to reinstate them on their unconditional application for reinstatement, even if their jobs have been filled. Therefore, the employer must dismiss strike replacements to make room for the returning strikers.

Replacements hired after the date the strike was converted into an unfair labor practice strike must also be discharged if necessary to make room for the returning strikers. At this point the employer should again be reminded of the impact of the recent Belknap decision, supra, as it relates to "permanent" replacement rights. Namely, employees who were promised "permanent" employment may have a breach of contract claim should the employee be terminated as a result of an unfair labor practice reinstatement order by the NLRB. This could expose the employer to double pay - for the returning strikers and for the replacements.

Significantly, an employer may refuse to reinstate an unfair labor practice striker under limited circumstances.

In particular, an employer is justified in refusing to reinstate an employee who has engaged in serious strike misconduct. In deciding whether to reinstate an unfair labor practice striker guilty of unprotected misconduct, the NLRB will generally balance the severity of the striker misconduct against the severity of the employer's unfair labor practices.

2. Replacement Workers.

The job retention rights of replacement workers also differ according to the type of strike which resulted in their employment in the first instance (i.e., economic or unfair labor practice). Accordingly, the employer may not be forced to discharge a replacement who was hired as a result of an economic strike even though these strikers may periodically make an unconditional offer to return to their old position. On the other hand, unfair labor practice strikers are given an unconditional right to reinstatement. Therefore, temporary replacements must be dismissed if the position can be filled by a reinstated employee. Permanent replacements are also subject to dismissal if unfair labor practice strikers return to work. However, these "permanent" replacements may also have a breach of contract claim resulting from their dismissal. Belknap, supra.

F.   Decertification/Deauthorization.

Decertification of the union is always a post-strike consideration especially when replacements have been hired to work during the strike. The reason for this is that the replacement workers are eligible to vote in the next NLRB election. The union's authority to bargain for a unit of employees will be rescinded upon a timely vote by the majority of employees in the union that they do not wish to be represented by that union.

Deauthorization of the striking union is also a possibility after resolution of the labor dispute. This entails an election held by the NLRB in which employees are polled on whether they wish to rescind the authority of their bargaining agent to acquire union dues deductions under a union-shop contract. The union-shop clause becomes invalid immediately upon the NLRB's determination that a majority of the employees have voted to rescind the authority. One result of a successful deauthorization is the rescission of the employer's duty to provide union dues check-off pursuant to the union-security clause. Decertifications and deauthorizations are sometimes motivators in management's mind when the decision to take a strike is made.

G. Personnel Policies.

Once the strike is resolved and the parties have returned to normalcy, it is a good idea for management to review its personnel policies. The cause of the dispute may have involved a misunderstanding over the existing policies. Therefore, management may wish to consider revising its present personnel program. A number of considerations can be addressed by the company's personnel committee. For example, are the company's present policies clearly written and usually understood by employees? Is the company enforcing the policies it now has? Are the present policies being enforced uniformly throughout the company? Do the company's supervisors do a good job of interpreting policies for employees? Has the company reviewed its competitor's policies? Is the company competitive with others in the area? Finally, does the company have a good procedure for disseminating policies? The recent strike activity may have been initiated by a misunderstanding of the employer's present policies or lack of them. At the same time, management should carefully review

-142-

its no-solicitation/no-distribution policy in light of recent legal developments. Management should revise or implement amended personnel policies to correct these deficiencies.

H. <u>Duty to Bargain During the Strike.</u>

The mere fact that employees are on strike is not an excuse for a refusal to bargain with the union. An impasse in the bargaining negotiations that would otherwise relieve an employer from bargaining is broken by a strike, and thereafter the employer is under a duty to resume negotiations, but the employer is not under a duty to initiate a method for settling the strike.

A refusal to bargain with a striking union that represents the employees is not only an unfair labor practice, but it also could convert an economic strike into an unfair practice strike. This situation may arise when an employer unilaterally withdraws its pre-strike proposals and repudiates any pre-strike agreements. By such conduct, the employer may commit unfair labor practices and lose the right to deny reinstatement to the strikers on the grounds that replacements have been hired.

On the other hand, an employer who has bargained with the union in good faith and has not engaged in an unfair labor practice may be able to timely contest the majority status of a union during or following an economic strike, provided the objective consideration justify a reasonable doubt of continued majority status.

I. Bringing an End to the Strife and Controversy.

The actual resolution of the strike depends on a number of circumstances. First, for any possiblity of settlement to exist there must be a willingness by both parties to listen and compromise. Additionally, the influence of mediation and public opinion may force the parties to hammer out their differences.

Prior to a settlement, the union may wish to take stock of the overall situation and determine whether or not it would be in its best interest to drop its demands and return to work. Accordingly, management may also undertake the same weighing process. The employer will also determine whether it is in the best interests of the company to accede to the union's demands. Eventually, the strike is resolved in some fashion. However, this does not bring an end to the discontent and bitterness which may still exist between the various factions. Harmonious working relationships can only be achieved by a mutual desire to promote a peaceful adjustment. This effort requires a willingness to put aside inconsequential differences while avoiding rehashing any picket line conflict. Only by mutual respect for each other's position can the parties truly bring an end to the strife and controversy.

Once the strike is resolved, management should review the actions taken to resolve each major problem that arose, what was successful, what proved ineffective and what remedies were used. This debriefing session should include members of the strike management team, department heads and supervisors. During this meeting, a summary of the strike and recommendations for improvements should be elicited for the future avoidance of the recent dispute.

J. Conclusion.

General Sherman said, "War is hell." If a strike is economic warfare between management and labor, it, too, bears its hellish aspects. Organized labor has often waged strikes aggressively and confidently and has used whatever means available to achieve its goals. The union will seek allies: other nonstriking employees and other unions. The union may try to enlist the aid of the NLRB. The union may try to pressure neutral suppliers and customers into joining their camp. Management should do likewise. Management should also try to use administrative and judicial processes to strengthen its position and to seek the support of public opinion. The unprepared nation that wages war will either lose or suffer significant losses before the final victory is achieved. So, too, unprepared management will face losses if it encounters a strike with no plan in mind and if it lacks the will to use all available economic and legal weapons to parry the union's thrusts. Only in this way will management ever achieve its goal of successfully concluding the strike.

WORK STOPPAGES BY REGION
JANUARY - JUNE 1983

REGION	NUMBER
Middle Atlantic	113
North Central	60
West Coast	30
New England	27
Midwest	20
Mid-South	15
Southwest	11
Rocky Mountain	3
Multiple Region	5

WORK STOPPAGES
JANUARY - JUNE, 1983

MONTH	NUMBER STARTING	NUMBER IN PROGRESS[1]
January	34	62
February	40	66
March	65	92
April	44	63
May	59	67
June	18	22

[1]Represents minimum number in progress. Where end date is not known, stoppage is not counted beyond month started. Work stoppage date computed through June 15, 1983.

WORK STOPPAGES* BY UNION
JANUARY - JUNE, 1983

UNION	NUMBER	UNION	NUMBER
IBT	69	IUOE	13
UFCW	30	IAM	11
UAW	27	IBEW	11
USE	19	LIUNA	8
IUE	17	ANA	8
SEIU	14	HERE	7

*Number represents reported work stoppages where each listed union is involved. Unions involved in fewer than seven stoppages are not represented here. Some stoppages may have begun before January 1, 1983.

BNA's Labor Economic Report, Bureau of National Affairs, Inc. (1983)

APPENDIX A-1

LABOR ECONOMIC DATA BY INDUSTRY
JANUARY - JUNE, 1983

MANUFACTURING INDUSTRIES	INCIDENTS OF WORK STOPPAGE	NONMANUFACTURING & SERVICE INDUSTRIES	INCIDENTS OF WORK STOPPAGE
Chemicals	6	Apparel, Retail	*
Food & Beverage, Prepared	29	Apparel, Wholesale	*
Furniture	*	Communications Services	3
Glass/Clay/Stone Products	5	Department Stores	1
Instruments	2	Entertainment Services	4
Leather & Leather Products	*	Food --	
Lumber & Lumber Products	1	-Raw, Crops	*
Machinery --		-Raw, Livestock	*
-Commercial/Industrial Electrical	23	-Restaurants & Bars	2
-Communications Equip.	*	-Retail Food & Beverage	17
-Computers & Related Parts	*	-Wholesale Food & Beverage	13
-Consumer/Household Electrical	*	Hotels & Motels	6
-Industrial/Nonelectrical	18	Mining --	
-Oil Field Equipment	1	-Coal, All Types	*
Metals --		-Glass/Clay/Stone, Raw	2
-Fabricated Metals	18	-Oil & Gas Drilling	1
-Primary Metalworks, Nonsteel	6	-Ore Mining	*
-Primary Steel Production	7	-Other Nonmetallics	*
Paper & Paper Products	5	Organizations	6
Petroleum Refining & Products	*	Professional Services --	
Printing & Publishing	8	-Computer Software Services	*
Rubber & Rubber Products	3	-Health Services	16
Textiles --		-Monetary Services	1
-Finished Apparel & Textiles	4	-Misc. Professional Services	4
-Mill Goods	*	Transportation Services --	
Tobacco Products	*	-Air Freight	3
Transportation Equipment --		-Air Passenger	1
-Aircraft	1	-Local Transportation	3
-Autos & Trucks	5	-Marine Transportation	*
-Rail Equipment	*	-Rail Services, Nonlocal	*
-Ships & Boats	1	-Trucking Services	10
-Misc. Transportation Equipment	*	-Transportation Repair, All Types	*
Miscellaneous Manufacturing	2	-Misc. Transportation Services	*
		Utilities, Nonpublic	5
		Misc. Commercial Services	9
		Misc. Consumer Services	2
		Misc. Retail Stores	3
		Misc. Wholesale Distributors	5
		Misc. Nonmanufacturing	*
		Total Nonmanufacturing & Services	117
Total Manufacturing	145	Total Manufacturing	145
		Total All Industries	262[1]

*=No reported incidents

[1]Construction industry work stoppages not listed here. Work stoppage data computed through June 15, 1983.

BNA's Labor Economic Report, Bureau of National Affairs, Inc. (1983)

APPENDIX A-2

NATIONAL LABOR RELATIONS BOARD

RIGHTS OF EMPLOYEES

SEC. 7. Employees shall have the right to self-organization, to form, join, or assist labor organizations, to bargain collectively through representatives of their own choosing, and to engage in other concerted activities for the purpose of collective bargaining or other mutual aid or protection, and shall also have the right to refrain from any or all of such activities except to the extent that such right may be affected by an agreement requiring membership in a labor organization as a condition of employment as authorized in section 8(a)(3).

UNFAIR LABOR PRACTICES

SEC. 8. (a) It shall be an unfair labor practice for an employer—

(1) to interfere with, restrain, or coerce employees in the exercise of the rights guaranteed in section 7;

(2) to dominate or interfere with the formation or administration of any labor organization or contribute financial or other support to it: *Provided*, That subject to rules and regulations made and published by the Board pursuant to section 6, an employer shall not be prohibited from permitting employees to confer with him during working hours without loss of time or pay;

(3) by discrimination in regard to hire or tenure of employment or any term or condition of employment to encourage or discourage membership in any labor organization: *Provided*, That nothing in this Act, or in any other statute of the United States, shall preclude an employer from making an agreement with a labor organization (not established, maintained, or assisted by any action defined in section 8(a) of this Act as an unfair labor practice) to require as a condition of employment membership therein on or after the thirtieth day following the beginning of such employment or the effective date of such agreement, whichever is the later, (i) if such labor organization is the representative of the employees as provided in section 9(a), in the appropriate collective-bargaining unit covered by such agreement when made, and (ii) unless following an election held as provided in section 9(e) within one year preceding the effective date of such agreement, the Board shall have certified that at least a majority of the employees eligible to vote in such election have voted to rescind the authority of such labor organization to make such an agreement: *Provided further*, That no employer shall justify any discrimination against an employee for non-membership in a labor organization (A) if he has reasonable grounds for believing that such membership was not available to the employee on the same terms and conditions generally applicable to other members, or (B) if he has reasonable grounds for believing that membership was denied or terminated for reasons other than the failure of the employee to tender the periodic dues and the initiation fees uniformly required as a condition of acquiring or retaining membership;

(4) to discharge or otherwise discriminate against an employee because he has filed charges or given testimony under this Act;

(5) to refuse to bargain collectively with the representatives of his employees, subject to the provisions of section 9(a).

(b) It shall be an unfair labor practice for a labor organization or its agents—

(1) to restrain or coerce (A) employees in the exercise of the rights guaranteed in section 7: *Provided*, That this paragraph shall not impair the right of a labor organization to prescribe its own rules with respect to the acquisition or retention of membership therein; or (B) an employer in the selection of his representatives for the purposes of collective bargaining or the adjustment of grievances;

(2) to cause or attempt to cause an employer to discriminate against an employee in violation of subsection (a)(3) or to discriminate against an employee with respect to whom membership in such organization has been denied or terminated on some ground other than his failure to tender the periodic dues and the initiation fees uniformly required as a condition of acquiring or retaining membership;

(3) to refuse to bargain collectively with an employer, provided it is the representative of his employees subject to the provisions of section 9(a);

(4) (i) to engage in, or to induce or encourage any individual employed by any person engaged in commerce or in an industry affecting commerce to engage in, a strike or a refusal in the course of his employment to use, manufacture, process, transport, or otherwise handle or work on any goods, articles, materials, or commodities or to perform any services; or (ii) to threaten, coerce, or restrain any person engaged in commerce or in an industry affecting commerce, where in either case an object thereof is:

(A) forcing or requiring any employer or self-employed person to join any labor or employer organization or to enter into any agreement which is prohibited by section 8(e);

(B) forcing or requiring any person to cease using, selling, handling, transporting, or otherwise dealing in the products of any other producer, processor, or manufacturer, or to cease doing business with any other person, or forcing or requiring any other employer to recognize or bargain with a labor organization as the representative of his employees unless such labor organization has been certified as the representative of such employees under the provisions of section 9: *Provided,* That nothing contained in this clause (B) shall be construed to make unlawful, where not otherwise unlawful, any primary strike or primary picketing;

(C) forcing or requiring any employer to recognize or bargain with a particular labor organization as the representative of his employees if another labor organization has been certified as the representative of such employees under the provisions of section 9;

(D) forcing or requiring any employer to assign particular work to employees in a particular labor organization or in a particular trade, craft, or class rather than to employees in another labor organization or in another trade, craft, or class, unless such employer is failing to conform to an order or certification of the Board determining the bargaining representative for employees performing such work:

Provided, That nothing contained in this subsection (b) shall be construed to make unlawful a refusal by any person to enter upon the premises of any employer (other than his own employer), if the employees of such employer are engaged in a strike ratified or approved by a representative of such employees whom such employer is required to recognize under this Act: *Provided further,* That for the purposes of this paragraph (4) only, nothing contained in such paragraph shall be construed to prohibit publicity, other than picketing, for the purpose of truthfully advising the public, including consumers and members of a labor organization, that a product or products are produced by an employer with whom the labor organization has a primary dispute and are distributed by another employer, as long as such publicity does not have an effect of inducing any individual employed by any person other than the primary employer in the course of his employment to refuse to pick up, deliver, or transport any goods, or not to perform any services, at the establishment of the employer engaged in such distribution;

(5) to require of employees covered by an agreement authorized under

subsection (a)(3) the payment, as a condition precedent to becoming a member of such organization, of a fee in an amount which the Board finds excessive or discriminatory under all the circumstances. In making such a finding, the Board shall consider, among other relevant factors, the practices and customs of labor organizations in the particular industry, and the wages currently paid to the employees affected;

(6) to cause or attempt to cause an employer to pay or deliver or agree to pay or deliver any money or other thing of value, in the nature of an exaction, for services which are not performed or not to be performed; and

(7) to picket or cause to be picketed, or threaten to picket or cause to be picketed, any employer where an object thereof is forcing or requiring an employer to recognize or bargain with a labor organization as the representative of his employees, or forcing or requiring the employees of an employer to accept or select such labor organization as their collective bargaining representative, unless such labor organization is currently certified as the representative of such employees:

(A) where the employer has lawfully recognized in accordance with this Act any other labor organization and a question concerning representation may not appropriately be raised under section 9(c) of this Act,

(B) where within the preceding twelve months a valid election under section 9(c) of this Act has been conducted, or

(C) where such picketing has been conducted without a petition under section 9(c) being filed within a reasonable period of time not to exceed thirty days from the commencement of such picketing: *Provided*, That when such a petition has been filed the Board shall forthwith, without regard to the provisions of section 9(c)(1) or the absence of a showing of a substantial interest on the part of the labor organization, direct an election in such unit as the Board finds to be appropriate and shall certify the results thereof: *Provided further*, That nothing in this subparagraph (C) shall be construed to prohibit any picketing or other publicity for the purpose of truthfully advising the public (including consumers) that an employer does not employ members of, or have a contract with, a labor organization, unless an effect of such picketing is to induce any individual employed by any other person in the course of his employment, not to pick up, deliver or transport any goods or not to perform any services.

Nothing in this paragraph (7) shall be construed to permit any act which would otherwise be an unfair labor practice under this section 8(b).

(c) The expressing of any views, argument, or opinion, or the dissemination thereof, whether in written, printed, graphic, or visual form, shall not constitute or be evidence of an unfair labor practice under any of the provisions of this Act, if such expression contains no threat of reprisal or force or promise of benefit.

(d) For the purposes of this section, to bargain collectively is the performance of the mutual obligation of the employer and the representative of the employees to meet at reasonable times and confer in good faith with respect to wages, hours, and other terms and conditions of employment, or the negotiation of an agreement, or any question arising thereunder, and the execution of a written contract incorporating any agreement reached if requested by either party, but such obligation does not compel either party to agree to a proposal or require the making of a concession: *Provided*, That where there is in effect a collective-bargaining contract covering employees in an industry affecting commerce, the duty to bargain collectively shall also mean that no party to such contract shall terminate or modify such contract, unless the party desiring such termination or modification—

(1) serves a written notice upon the other party to the contract of the proposed termination or modification sixty days prior to the expiration date thereof, or in the event such contract contains no expiration date, sixty days prior to the time it is proposed to make such termination or modification;

(2) offers to meet and confer with the other party for the purpose of negotiating a new contract or a contract containing the proposed modifications;

(3) notifies the Federal Mediation and Conciliation Service within thirty days after such notice of the existence of a dispute, and simultaneously therewith notifies any State or Territorial agency established to mediate and conciliate disputes within the State or Territory where the dispute occurred, provided no agreement has been reached by that time; and

(4) continues in full force and effect, without resorting to strike or lock-out, all the terms and conditions of the existing contract for a period of sixty days after such notice is given or until the expiration date of such contract, whichever occurs later:

The duties imposed upon employers, employees, and labor organizations by paragraphs (2), (3), and (4) shall become inapplicable upon an intervening certification of the Board, under which the labor organization or individual, which is a party to the contract, has been superseded as or ceased to be the representative of the employees subject to the provisions of section 9(a), and the duties so imposed shall not be construed as requiring either party to discuss or agree to any modification of the terms and conditions contained in a contract for a fixed period, if such modification is to become effective before such terms and conditions can be reopened under the provisions of the contract. Any employee who engages in a strike within any notice* period specified in this subsection, or who engages in any strike within the appropriate period specified in subsection (g) of this section* shall lose his status as an employee of the employer engaged in the particular labor dispute, for the purposes of sections 8, 9, and 10 of this Act, as amended, but such loss of status for such employee shall terminate if and when he is reemployed by such employer. Whenever the collective bargaining involves employees of a health care institution, the provisions of this section 8(d) shall be modified as follows:

(A) The notice of section 8(d)(1) shall be ninety days; the notice of section 8(d)(3) shall be sixty days; and the contract period of section 8(d)(4) shall be ninety days;

(B) Where the bargaining is for an initial agreement following certification or recognition, at least thirty days' notice of the existence of a dispute shall be given by the labor organization to the agencies set forth in section 8(d)(3).

(C) After notice is given to the Federal Mediation and Conciliation Service under either clause (A) or (B) of this sentence, the Service shall promptly communicate with the parties and use its best efforts, by mediation and conciliation, to bring them to agreement. The parties shall participate fully and promptly in such meetings as may be undertaken by the Service for the purpose of aiding in a settlement of the dispute.*

(e) It shall be an unfair labor practice for any labor organization and any employer to enter into any contract or agreement, express or implied, whereby such employer ceases or refrains or agrees to cease or refrain from handling, using, selling, transporting or otherwise dealing in any of the products of any other employer, or

---

* Pursuant to Public Law 93-360, 93d Cong., S. 3203, 88 Stat. 396, the last sentence of Sec. 8(d) is amended by striking the words "the sixty day" and inserting the words "any notice" and by inserting before the words "shall lose" the phrase ", or who engages in any strike within the appropriate period specified in subsection (g) of this section." In addition, the end of paragraph Sec. 8(d) is amended by adding a new sentence "Whenever the collective bargaining . . . aiding in a settlement of the dispute."

to cease doing business with any other person, and any contract or agreement entered into heretofore or hereafter containing such an agreement shall be to such extent unenforceable and void: *Provided,* That nothing in this subsection (e) shall apply to an agreement between a labor organization and an employer in the construction industry relating to the contracting or subcontracting of work to be done at the site of the construction, alteration, painting, or repair of a building, structure, or other work: *Provided further,* That for the purposes of this subsection (e) and section 8(b)(4)(B) the terms "any employer", "any person engaged in commerce or in industry affecting commerce", and "any person" when used in relation to the terms "any other producer, processor, or manufacturer", "any other employer", or "any other person" shall not include persons in the relation of a jobber, manufacturer, contractor, or sub-contractor working on the goods or premises of the jobber or manufacturer or performing parts of an integrated process of production in the apparel and clothing industry: *Provided further,* That nothing in this Act shall prohibit the enforcement of any agreement which is within the foregoing exception.

(f) It shall not be an unfair labor practice under subsections (a) and (b) of this section for an employer engaged primarily in the building and construction industry to make an agreement covering employees engaged (or who, upon their employment, will be engaged) in the building and construction industry with a labor organization of which building and construction employees are members (not established, maintained, or assisted by any action defined in section 8(a) of this Act as an unfair labor practice) because (1) the majority status of such labor organization has not been established under the provisions of section 9 of this Act prior to the making of such agreement, or (2) such agreement requires as a condition of employment, membership in such labor organization after the seventh day following the beginning of such employment or the effective date of the agreement, whichever is later, or (3) such agreement requires the employer to notify such labor organization of opportunities for employment with such employer, or gives such labor organization an opportunity to refer qualified applicants for such employment, or (4) such agreement specifies minimum training or experience qualifications for employment or provides for priority in opportunities for employment based upon length of service with such employer, in the industry or in the particular geographical area: *Provided,* That nothing in this subsection shall set aside the final proviso to section 8(a)(3) of this Act: *Provided further,* That any agreement which would be invalid, but for clause (1) of this subsection, shall not be a bar to a petition filed pursuant to section 9(c) or 9(e).*

(g) A labor organization before engaging in any strike, picketing, or other concerted refusal to work at any health care institution shall, not less than ten days prior to such action, notify the institution in writing and the Federal Mediation and Conciliation Service of that intention, except that in the case of bargaining for an initial agreement following certification or recognition the notice required by this subsection shall not be given until the expiration of the period specified in clause (B) of the last sentence of section 8(d) of this Act. The notice shall state the date and time that such action will commence. The notice, once given, may be extended by the written agreement of both parties.**

---

*Sec. 8(f) is inserted in the Act by subsec. (a) of Sec. 705 of Public Law 86–257. Sec. 705(b) provides:

Nothing contained in the amendment made by subsection (a) shall be construed as authorizing the execution or application of agreements requiring membership in a labor organization as a condition of employment in any State or Territory in which such execution or application is prohibited by State or Territorial law.

**Pursuant to Public Law 93–360, 93d Cong., S. 3203, 88 Stat. 396. Sec. 8 is amended by adding subsection (g).

TITLE II—CONCILIATION OF LABOR DISPUTES IN INDUSTRIES AFFECTING COMMERCE; NATIONAL EMERGENCIES

SEC. 201. That it is the policy of the United States that—

(a) sound and stable industrial peace and the advancement of the general welfare, health, and safety of the Nation and of the best interest of employers and employees can most satisfactorily be secured by the settlement of issues between employers and employees through the processes of conference and collective bargaining between employers and the representatives of their employees:

(b) the settlement of issues between employers and employees through collective bargaining may be advanced by making available full and adequate governmental facilities for conciliation, mediation, and voluntary arbitration to aid and encourage employers and the representatives of their employees to reach and maintain agreements concerning rates of pay, hours, and working conditions, and to make all reasonable efforts to settle their differences by mutual agreement reached through conferences and collective bargaining or by such methods as may be provided for in any applicable agreement for the settlement of disputes; and

(c) certain controversies which arise between parties to collective-bargaining agreements may be avoided or minimized by making available full and adequate governmental facilities for furnishing assistance to employers and the representatives of their employees in formulating for inclusion within such agreements provision for adequate notice of any proposed changes in the terms of such agreements, for the final adjustment of grievances or questions regarding the application or interpretation of such agreements, and other provisions designed to prevent the subsequent arising of such controversies.

SEC. 202. (a) There is hereby created an independent agency to be known as the Federal Mediation and Conciliation Service (herein referred to as the "Service," except that for sixty days after the date of the enactment of this Act such term shall refer to the Conciliation Service of the Department of Labor). The Service shall be under the direction of a Federal Mediation and Conciliation Director (hereinafter referred to as the "Director"), who shall be appointed by the President by and with the advice and consent of the Senate. The Director shall receive compensation at the rate of $12,000* per annum. The Director shall not engage in any other business, vocation, or employment.

(b) The Director is authorized, subject to the civil-service laws, to appoint such clerical and other personnel as may be necessary for the execution of the functions of the Service, and shall fix their compensation in accordance with the Classification Act of 1923, as amended, and may, without regard to the provisions of the civil-service laws and the Classification Act of 1923, as amended, appoint and fix the compensation of such conciliators and mediators as may be necessary to carry out the functions of the Service. The Director is authorized to make such expenditures

---

*Pursuant to Public Law 90-206, 90th Cong., 81 Stat. 644, approved Dec. 16, 1967, and in accordance with Sec. 225(f)(ii) thereof, effective in 1969, the salary of the Director shall be $40,000 per year.

for supplies, facilities, and services as he deems necessary. Such expenditures shall be allowed and paid upon presentation of itemized vouchers therefor approved by the Director or by any employee designated by him for that purpose.

(c) The principal office of the Service shall be in the District of Columbia, but the Director may establish regional offices convenient to localities in which labor controversies are likely to arise. The Director may by order, subject to revocation at any time, delegate any authority and discretion conferred upon him by this Act to any regional director, or other officer or employee of the Service. The Director may establish suitable procedures for cooperation with State and local mediation agencies. The Director shall make an annual report in writing to Congress at the end of the fiscal year.

(d) All mediation and conciliation functions of the Secretary of Labor or the United States Conciliation Service under section 8 of the Act entitled "An Act to create a Department of Labor," approved March 4, 1913 (U.S.C., title 29, sec. 51), and all functions of the United States Conciliation Service under any other law are hereby transferred to the Federal Mediation and Conciliation Service, together with the personnel and records of the United States Conciliation Service. Such transfer shall take effect upon the sixtieth day after the date of enactment of this Act. Such transfer shall not affect any proceedings pending before the United States Conciliation Service or any certification, order, rule, or regulation theretofore made by it or by the Secretary of Labor. The Director and the Service shall not be subject in any way to the jurisdiction or authority of the Secretary of labor or any official or division of the Department of Labor.

FUNCTIONS OF THE SERVICE

SEC. 203. (a) It shall be the duty of the Service, in order to prevent or minimize interruptions of the free flow of commerce growing out of labor disputes, to assist parties to labor disputes in industries affecting commerce to settle such disputes through conciliation and mediation.

(b) The Service may proffer its services in any labor dispute in any industry affecting commerce, either upon its own motion or upon the request of one or more of the parties to the dispute, whenever in its judgment such dispute threatens to cause a substantial interruption of commerce. The Director and the Service are directed to avoid attempting to mediate disputes which would have only a minor effect on interstate commerce if State or other conciliation services are available to the parties. Whenever the Service does proffer its services in any dispute, it shall be the duty of the Service promptly to put itself in communication with the parties and to use its best efforts, by mediation and conciliation, to bring them to agreement.

(c) If the Director is not able to bring the parties to agreement by conciliation within a reasonable time, he shall seek to induce the parties voluntarily to seek other means of settling the dispute without resort to strike, lock-out, or other coercion, including submission to the employees in the bargaining unit of the employer's last offer of settlement for approval or rejection in a secret ballot. The failure or refusal of either party to agree to any procedure suggested by the Director shall not be deemed a violation of any duty or obligation imposed by this Act.

(d) Final adjustment by a method agreed upon by the parties is hereby declared to be the desirable method for settlement of grievance disputes arising over the application or interpretation of an existing collective-bargaining agreement. The Service is directed to make its conciliation and mediation services available in the settlement of such grievance disputes only as a last resort and in exceptional cases.

Sec. 204. (a) In order to prevent or minimize interruptions of the free flow of commerce growing out of labor disputes, employers and employees and their representatives, in any industry affecting commerce, shall—

(1) exert every reasonable effort to make and maintain agreements concerning rates of pay, hours, and working conditions, including provision for adequate notice of any proposed change in the terms of such agreements;

(2) whenever a dispute arises over the terms or application of a collective-bargaining agreement and a conference is requested by a party or prospective party thereto, arrange promptly for such a conference to be held and endeavor in such conference to settle such dispute expeditiously; and

(3) in case such dispute is not settled by conference, participate fully and promptly in such meetings as may be undertaken by the Service under this Act for the purpose of aiding in a settlement of the dispute.

Sec. 205. (a) There is hereby created a National Labor-Management Panel which shall be composed of twelve members appointed by the President, six of whom shall be selected from among persons outstanding in the field of management and six of whom shall be selected from among persons outstanding in the field of labor. Each member shall hold office for a term of three years, except that any member appointed to fill a vacancy occurring prior to the expiration of the term for which his predecessor was appointed shall be appointed for the remainder of such term, and the terms of office of the members first taking office shall expire, as designated by the President at the time of appointment, four at the end of the first year, four at the end of the second year, and four at the end of the third year after the date of appointment. Members of the panel, when serving on business of the panel, shall be paid compensation at the rate of $25 per day, and shall also be entitled to receive an allowance for actual and necessary travel and subsistence expenses while so serving away from their places of residence.

(b) It shall be the duty of the panel, at the request of the Director, to advise in the avoidance of industrial controversies and the manner in which mediation and voluntary adjustment shall be administered, particularly with reference to controversies affecting the general welfare of the country.

TITLE III

SUITS BY AND AGAINST LABOR ORGANIZATIONS

SEC. 301. (a) Suits for violation of contracts between an employer and a labor organization representing employees in an industry affecting commerce as defined in this Act, or between any such labor organizations, may be brought in any district court of the United States having jurisdiction of the parties, without respect to the amount in controversy or without regard to the citizenship of the parties.

(b) Any labor organization which represents employees in an industry affecting commerce as defined in this Act and any employer whose activities affect commerce as defined in this Act shall be bound by the acts of its agents. Any such labor organization may sue or be sued as an entity and in behalf of the employees whom it represents in the courts of the United States. Any money judgment against a labor organization in a district court of the United States shall be enforceable only against the organization as an entity and against its assets, and shall not be enforceable against any individual member or his assets.

(c) For the purposes of actions and proceedings by or against labor organizations in the district courts of the United States, district courts shall be deemed to have jurisdiction of a labor organization (1) in the district in which such organization maintains its principal offices, or (2) in any district in which its duly authorized officers or agents are engaged in representing or acting for employee members.

(d) The service of summons, subpena, or other legal process of any court of the United States upon an officer or agent of a labor organization, in his capacity as such, shall constitute service upon the labor organization.

(e) For the purposes of this section, in determining whether any person is acting as an "agent" of another person so as to make such other person responsible for his acts, the question of whether the specific acts performed were actually authorized or subsequently ratified shall not be controlling.

Cover Letter

(Current Date)

VIA CERTIFIED MAIL
RETURN RECEIPT REQUESTED

Name
President
Local Union
Address
City, State Zip Code

     Re: Contract Negotiations

Dear _____:

Pursuant to Article XXXVI of the collective bargaining
agreement and to Section 8(d) of NLRA, this is to notify
you that we propose to terminate or modify the collective
bargaining agreement presently enforced between Employer
and your labor organization on or before _____.
Such termination or modification may occur with regard to
wages, hours and other terms and conditions of employment
of employees represented by your labor organization.

Employer offers to meet and confer with you and other duly-
designated representatives of the Union for the purpose of
negotiating a new collective bargaining agreement. Please
contact the undersigned for the purposes of arranging a
time and meeting to commence such negotiations.

     Very truly yours,

     [To Be Signed By The Chief
     Spokesman For Employer]

Enc.: Copy of Notice to Mediation Agencies:
     Federal Mediation and Conciliation Service
     State Mediation Agency

     (Use FMCS Form F-7)
     See C-2 for sample

                 APPENDIX C-1

* U.S. GOVERNMENT PRINTING OFFICE: 1982-388-856

FMCS FORM F-7
REVISED JULY 82

FORM APPROVED
OMB NO. D23-R00 10

NOTICE TO MEDIATION AGENCIES

DIVISION OF CASE CONTROL

TO: **FEDERAL MEDIATION AND CONCILIATION SERVICE** AND APPROPRIATE STATE OR TERRITORIAL AGENCY
2100 K STREET, N.W.
WASHINGTON, D.C. 20427

You are hereby notified that written notice of the proposed termination or modification of the existing collective bargaining contract was served upon the other party to this contract and that no agreement has been reached.

① NAME OF EMPLOYER

② CONTRACT EXPIRATION OR REOPENING DATE →

③ NAME OF UNION AND LOCAL NO.

④ CITY, STATE AND ZIP CODE OF EFFECTED ESTABLISHMENT

⑤ STREET ADDRESS OF EMPLOYER — CITY — STATE — ZIP

⑥ STREET ADDRESS OF UNION — CITY — STATE — ZIP

⑦ EMPLOYER OFFICIAL TO CONTACT — ⑧ A.C. PHONE

⑨ TOTAL NUMBER EMPLOYED AT EFFECTED LOCATION(S)

⑩ UNION OFFICIAL TO CONTACT — ⑪ A.C. PHONE

⑫ NUMBER OF EMPLOYEES COVERED BY CONTRACT

⑬ INDUSTRY — ⑭ PRINCIPAL PRODUCT OR SERVICE

⑮ THIS NOTICE IS FILED ON BEHALF OF (x) ☐ UNION   ☐ EMPLOYER

⑯ NAME AND TITLE OF OFFICIAL FILING THIS NOTICE

⑰ SIGNATURE AND DATE

⑱ STREET — CITY — STATE — ZIP

Receipt of this notice does not constitute a request for mediation nor does it commit the agencies to offer their facilities. This particular form of notice is not legally required. Receipt of notice will not be acknowledged in writing by the Federal Mediation and Conciliation Service.

NO. 1 ORIGINAL · To F.M.C.S.

APPENDIX C-2

A MESSAGE TO OUR EMPLOYEES, CUSTOMERS, SUPPLIERS, SHAREHOLDERS & FRIENDS FROM BRIGGS & STRATTON CORPORATION

Our final offer included:

$12.80/Hr. wages on average

$19.19/Hr. combined wages & benefits on average

$570/Mo. pension with 30 yr. service (minimum at end of contract term)

A New Profit Sharing Plan that includes minimum Cash payment of $2,250.00/person for the life of the contract

A New Company Stock Ownership Plan

Up to 7 weeks vacation

13 Paid Holidays

Fully Paid: Medical Plan　　Vision Care
**　　　　　　　Dental Plan　　Life Insurance**

On July 30, 1983 the union membership voted by a large margin to reject the company's three year contract proposal. Our Milwaukee area plants have been on strike since August 1st idling 7,800 employees. We regret the disruption this work stoppage has caused. We are issuing this release to correct misleading information including that now being given by individuals on television and radio talk shows.

BRIGGS & STRATTON'S BUSINESS ENVIRONMENT

Briggs & Stratton is being seriously challenged in both its engine business and automotive locks. Our automotive customers have demanded and received price reductions. In addition, future business is dependent upon further price cuts.

The threat to the engine business, which accounts for over 90% of our sales, has been even more severe. Domestic competitors have underpriced Briggs & Stratton to a greater extent each year. However, the major change in Briggs & Stratton's business has been the activity of Japanese competitors. In some countries, the Japanese, through their pricing, have captured large portions of the market. Honda, Yamaha, Kawasaki and Suzuki are all expanding rapidly in the small engine field. Honda is building a new factory in Japan to increase its engine capacity by over two million units. In addition, Honda has just announced plans to build a lawn mower plant in the United States (in North Carolina, not Wisconsin). Our Milwaukee area wages and benefits are more than 30% higher than those of our principal United States competitors and more than 50% higher than the Japanese competitors.

Our work force is one of the most productive in the United States. Visitors to our plants comment on the massiveness of our operations, the fine, well-kept appearance of our plants, but most of all, about the work pace and productivity of our employees. It has been this work pace, coupled with innovative engineering and financial commitments to manufacturing facilities, that has contributed greatly to our success.

We can, and intend, to pay our work force a premium wage. But we can no longer pay a 30% to 50% premium.

ISSUES RAISED BY THE UNION BARGAINING COMMITTEE PRIOR TO THE STRIKE

DIVIDENDS TO OUR SHAREHOLDERS — The present dividend rate of $1.58 per share is approximately a 5% return on the current stock price. Banks and Savings and Loan Associations pay almost double this rate. Yet the union repeatedly attacked our payment of dividends to shareholders, 35% of whom reside in Wisconsin.

PROFITABILITY OF THE COMPANY — Briggs & Stratton has achieved a good record of profitability. We are proud of this and we intend to remain profitable. Over the last five years, we have earned approximately $182 million. During these same years, we have reinvested, primarily in Milwaukee, $182 million for plant and equipment thus creating jobs.

ECONOMICS — The Company has offered to retain its current wage schedule which provides an average of $12.80 per hour in wages. Hiring rates for new employees would be reduced and the time for automatic increases would be lengthened from 65 weeks to 78 weeks. In addition to the $12.80 per hour wage rate the Company offered a profit sharing plan. Under this plan, up to 50% of the incremental profits would be available for profit sharing. As part of the profit sharing plan, the Company would pay in cash to eligible employees a minimum of $2,250.00 per person over the life of the contract. The Union Negotiating Committee rejected the Company's offer and made a counterproposal which the Company rejected. Since the strike began, the Union's chief negotiator now states that the economic demands of the Union are 3% in the second and third year of the contract.

PERSONAL DAYS — The company's offer has eliminated the personal days. The current vacation and holiday plans are among the finest in the community.

JOB PREFERENCE — (The ability of an employee to choose on a daily basis the job they wish to perform.) The Company's proposal would continue to allow employees virtually the same rights they now enjoy. There would be limitations on skilled trade and employees with less than five years seniority and additional time allowance for certain job preferences.

VOLUNTARY LAYOFF — (The right of the most senior people to choose to be laid off and collect unemployment benefits before new employees are laid off.) The Company does not like, but has agreed to allow employees to retain the right to voluntarily choose layoff. However, the Company is taking the position that employees with less than 18 months seniority be laid off before the most senior employees.

SUBCONTRACTING/MANAGEMENT RIGHTS — The Company has had a demand to give unlimited overtime to the skilled trades any time a single contractor is employed or a new die is being manufactured on the outside. The Company has always used outside contractors. They are needed to tool new products and processes. With the swiftness that the Japanese manufacturers can introduce new products and with our plans for new products, outside contractors will be even more important. We cannot, and will not, guarantee skilled employees unlimited overtime nor relinquish our rights to use alternate sources of supply.

OVERTIME — The Union insists on the right to not have to work even one Saturday of overtime on a mandatory basis.

SUMMARY — The Company's proposal was intended to retain jobs in Milwaukee. The only way a Company can retain jobs is to maintain its efficiency and remain competitive. Our past commitment to this area has been strong in terms of civic involvement, new jobs and capital spending. To date, the Union has chosen not to cooperate with these objectives.

BRIGGS & STRATTON CORPORATION

APPENDIX D

(To Be Typed On Employer Stationary)

(SAMPLE DISCIPLINARY NOTICE)

(Date)

<u>VIA CERTIFIED MAIL</u>
<u>RETURN RECEIPT REQUESTED</u>

Dear _____:

   It has come to our attention that you have engaged in picket line misconduct or other activities unprotected by law that could result in disciplinary action up to and including discharge.

   This matter is now under consideration. You will be informed when a decision is made concerning what disciplinary action, if any, will be taken against you.

                    Sincerely,

                                              APPENDIX E

SUGGESTED JOINT GUIDELINES FOR PICKETS

DURING A LABOR DISPUTE

(1) You have the constitutional right to picket peacefully. However, you will be subject to a fine for contempt of court if you continue to picket in violation of an injunction prohibiting picketing.

(2) Picketing will be allowed only in designated areas. This is necessary for your own safety and the safety of other members of the community.

(3) Unlawful activity will not be tolerated. Unlawful activity includes:

    (a) Blocking or obstructing the lawful use by any other person or persons of any private or public thoroughfares, property or of any positions of access or exit to or from any private or public building or dwelling (sidewalks, driveways, etc.).

    (b) Engaging in violent, abusive, indecent, profane, boisterous, unreasonably loud or otherwise disorderly conduct.

    (c) Preventing any person from engaging in or continuing in any lawful work or employment by threats, intimidation, force, or coercion of any kind.

    (d) Intentionally damaging property or causing bodily injury to any person.

    (e) Any conduct which tends to cause or provoke a disturbance.

    (f) Any assembly of three or more persons which causes such a disturbance of public order that it is reasonable to believe that the assembly will cause injury to persons or damage to property unless it is immediately dispersed.

APPENDIX F

SUGGESTED INSTRUCTIONS TO POLICE OFFICERS

AND SHERIFF DEPUTIES FOR PICKET LINE DUTY

(1)   Meet with pickets upon arrival at the picketing site to insure they are aware of the proper guidelines. Re-explain, if necessary, the plan you intend to follow. This should be done at the start of every new shift of pickets and will provide an opportunity to review recent developments or directives from command personnel.

(2)   Do not get involved in discussions regarding the issues causing the strike or picketing. However, maintain a cordial and friendly relationship with the public, other employees, and the pickets.

(3)   Make certain that, at all times, pickets remain in designated areas. Driveways, access sidewalks, and doors to buildings being picketed would never be blocked.

(4)   If vehicles approaching or leaving the picketed building threaten bodily injury to the pickets (not due to the fault of the pickets), call this to the attention of the employer. Make sure the employer has been briefed on the guidelines for picketing including his responsibilities.

(5)   Review the extent of your authority with your command officer.

(6)   Whenever possible, provide pickets with warnings that if prohibited activity continues arrests will occur.

(7)   Maintain accurate records of any and all incidents on the picket lines.

(8)   Brief the officer that relieves you regarding any problems or uncooperative pickets that have caused trouble on your tour of duty.

(9)   Don't make arrests as a show of force unless absolutely necessary.

APPENDIX G

Regional Director
National Labor Relations Board

            Re: F.O.I.A. Request:
                 Union Local ___

Dear Regional Director:

We are hereby making a request under the Freedom of Information
Act for the following with reference to the above-named Union.

    1. A listing of cases in the last five (5) years in
        which a complaint issued against Local ___ alleging
        a violation of Section 8(b)(1)(A) of the NLRA, speci-
        fically involving picket line misconduct or interfer-
        ence with the rights of non-striking employees.

    2. Copies of any decisions of the NLRB or Administrative
        Law Judge within the last five (5) years finding
        violations of Sec. 8(b)(1)(A) (picket line misconduct
        or interference).

    3. Copies of any contempt proceedings instituted by the
        NLRB within the last five (5) years against Local ___
        for action constituting violations of Sec. 8(b)(1)(A)
        and indication of the status of such proceedings.

We are willing to incur the cost associated with this request.
Please notify the undersigned if the anticipated cost will exceed
$_____. Thank you for you anticipated cooperation in this matter.

                                        APPENDIX H

)

PICKET LOG

Person Reporting: _____
Date: _____
Time: _____

1. Location_____

2. Date and time pickets put up_____

3. Number of employes picketing_____

4. Names of employes picketing_____

_____

_____

5. Number of Picket Signs and what does each say _____

_____

_____

_____

_____

6. Location of Pickets (give detail where they walk to and from)

_____

_____

_____

7. Date and Time Pickets removed _____

8. Names of all Union officers, agents, stewards on the picket

   line _____

SPECIAL REPORTS:

A.   A Special Report noting any change in the above facts
     each hour. If no changes, so indicate on report.

B.   A Special Report indicating date, time, names of individuals
     or firms not permitted entrance or exist from the plant or
     delayed.

C.   A special Report covering any unusual events, distrubances,
     damage to company property, unusual picket activity, etc.

All Special Reports are to be made within the hour of occurrence and
a copy delivered to the _____. _____
should be notified by telephone immediately.

APPENDIX I

INCIDENT REPORT

Your Name: _____ Date of Birth:__/__/__

Business and Home Address/Phone Numbers:_____

_____

Occupation:_____ Employed By:_____

Date of Occurrence:_____ Time:_____a.m.____ p.m.

Location:_____

Where were you?_____

_____

Names of other persons observing incident:_____

_____

Names of all Union officers, agents, stewards observing incident:

_____

_____

Explain in detail what you saw and heard (Give names of persons involved).

_____

_____

_____

_____

_____

_____

_____

_____

    I declare under penalty of perjury that the foregoing is true and correct.

Date: _____   _____
                                        Signature of Person Completing this Form

Date: _____   _____
                                        Witness to Signature

APPENDIX J

DAILY STAFFING REPORT

Instructions: List number of personnel on duty by category,
your comments re operations and return to
_____ by 5:00 p.m. each day.

_____

_____

Department, location and shift:_____

Normal personnel strength:_____

Your name and title:_____

_____

Personnel on Duty:

Number

_____
Departmental Regular

_____
Departmental Management and Supervisory

_____
Non-Departmental Regular

_____
Non-Departmental Management and Supervisory

_____
Non-Agency Replacements

_____
Community Volunteers

_____
Other

_____
Total

Comments: _____
_____
_____
_____
_____

Date: _____   _____
                                  Signature

APPENDIX K

DAILY WITHDRAWAL OF SERVICES

ABSENCE REPORT

Instructions: List all employees absent. This form must be filled
out and returned to _____
by 5:00 p.m. each day.

_____

_____

_____

_____

_____

_____

Department, location and shift:_____

Your name and title:_____

_____

_____ No employees were absent without officially approved leave.

_____ The employees listed below were absent from their normal
duty stations at the time indicated.

Name	Classification	Schedule duty period	Time/places where observed & remarks

Date:_____   _____
                                       Signature

APPENDIX L

Date: _____
Time: _____

RETURN FROM STRIKE INFORMATION SHEET

The purpose of this information sheet is to permit the Company to determine when the employer will reinstate you and to what job you will be reinstated.

COMPLETE THIS FORM CAREFULLY

If you do not understand any item, ask Management to explain the item to you. Falsification of any item will be grounds for discharge.

1. Name: _____
       First   Middle Initial   Last

2. Address: _____
       Number   Street   Apt. No.

3. Telephone Number: _____

4. Job Classification as of Date of Strike: _____

5. Job Assignment as of Date of Strike: _____

6. Seniority Date: _____

7. Shift as of Date of Strike: _____

I do hereby verify that the information provided above is correct to the best of my knowledge and hereby unconditionally apply for reinstatement to my job or a substantially equivalent job in the bargaining unit.

_____   _____
    Date   Signature

Company Witness:

_____   _____
    Date   Signature

_____

THE SPACE BELOW IS FOR COMPANY USE ONLY
(Any Comments Should Be Made on the Back of This Sheet)

Job Offered	Date & Time	Accepted	Refused	Initials
_____	_____	☐	☐	_____
_____	_____	☐	☐	_____
_____	_____	☐	☐	_____
_____	_____	☐	☐	_____

Time Card # _____   Issued On _____ By _____
                             Date   Initials

Reporting Time and Date: _____

APPENDIX M

RESIGNATION

_____
Name - Please Print

I, the undersigned, do state that I am hereby resigning as an employee of _____, effective _____. I further state that I have been advised that, by this resignation, I am giving up any right that I may have to reinstatement to active employment at

_____.

I further state that no pressure of any sort, either in the form of a threat or promise of benefit, has been exerted upon me to make such a resignation, and that I have done so of my own free will.

_____   _____
     Date   Signature

Witness:

_____   _____
     Date   Signature

APPENDIX N

<u>SAMPLE OFFER OF REINSTATEMENT</u>

DATE

<u>CERTIFIED MAIL/RETURN RECEIPT REQUESTED</u>

Employee's Name
Employee's Address

This letter will serve as an unconditional offer of reinstatement to your former position with XYZ Corporation, Inc.

Please report to work on _____.

By offering this reinstatement, we are not conceding that we owe you any back pay. If it is later determined by the National Labor Relations Board or any court that you are not protected by the National Labor Relations Act, we reserve the right to terminate your employment.

If there are any questions regarding these matters, please feel free to contact me.

Very truly yours,

XYZ Corporation, Inc.

cc: Name
      Field Examiner,
      National Labor Relations Board

      Name
      Compliance Officer,
      National Labor Relations Board

APPENDIX O

STRIKE COST CALCULATOR

6/80

① If your average weekly take home pay is:

	$200	220	240	260	280	300	320	340	360	380	400
② And following a strike, you get an HOURLY wage increase of: 20¢	25	27	30	32	35	37	40	42	45	47	50
25¢	20	22	24	26	28	30	32	34	36	38	40
30¢	16	18	20	21	23	25	26	28	30	31	33
35¢	14	15	17	18	20	21	22	24	25	27	28
40¢	12	13	15	16	17	18	20	21	22	23	25
45¢	11	12	13	14	15	16	17	18	20	21	22
50¢	10	11	12	13	14	15	16	17	18	19	20

③ You will have to work this many WEEKS, just to get back the earnings you lost in EACH WEEK of the strike.

As an example: If your take home pay is $200 per week and you get an hourly increase of 20¢ following a strike of one week, you would have to work 25 weeks just to get back your lost earnings!

Management Resources Association . . . . Milwaukee WI 53226

APPENDIX P